DAVID BOWIE

DAVID BOWIE
THE LAST INTERVIEW
and OTHER CONVERSATIONS

with an introduction by DENNIS JOHNSON

MELVILLE HOUSE
BROOKLYN · LONDON

DAVID BOWIE: THE LAST INTERVIEW
AND OTHER CONVERSATIONS

Copyright © 2016 by Melville House Publishing

Introduction © 2016 by Melville House Publishing, LLC

First Melville House printing: November 2016

"The First Interview" © 1964 by the BBC. Transcript made by Melville House Publishing from BBC television program *Tonight*, originally aired November 1964

"David Bowie Tells All and More" © 1973 by Patrick Salvo.
First published in *Interview*, March 1973

"Beat Godfather Meets Glitter MainMan" © 1973 by Craig Copetas.
First published in *Rolling Stone*, February 28, 1974

"David Bowie: Stardust Memories: Reflections on a Life of Wit and Style"
© 1987 by Kurt Loder. First published in *Rolling Stone*, April 23, 1987

"Bowie at the Bijou" © 1992 by *Movieline*, a publication of *Variety* and *Deadline*.
First published in *Movieline Magazine*, April 1, 1992

"Fashion: Turn to the Left; Fashion: Turn to the Right" © 2005 by
Dazed and Confused. First published in *Dazed and Confused*, November 1996

"*Bust*'s Interview with David Bowie" © 2000 by *Bust Magazine*. Originally
published by *Bust Magazine* as "*Bust*'s Interview with David Bowie," Fall 2000

"As the Artist Said to the Rock Star . . ." © 2001 by Tracey Emin.
First published in *The Guardian*, July 18, 2001

"The Last Interview" © 2006 by Ricky Gervais and Stephen Merchant.
Transcript made by Melville House Publishing from *Extras*, episode 8,
originally aired September 21, 2006

Every reasonable effort has been made to trace the owners of the copyright
for "The Raw and Uncut Interview," but this has proven impossible. The editors
and publishers will be glad to receive any information leading to more
complete acknowledgments for subsequent printings of this book.

Melville House Publishing
46 John Street   and
Brooklyn, NY 11201

8 Blackstock Mews
Islington
London N4 2BT

mhpbooks.com   facebook.com/mhpbooks   @melvillehouse

ISBN: 978-1-61219-575-9

Library of Congress Control Number: 2016953423

Printed in the United States of America
1   3   5   7   9   10   8   6   4   2

CONTENTS

INTRODUCTION

DENNIS JOHNSON

David Bowie gave a lot of interviews . . . until he didn't.

From the start of his career, he was regularly interviewed not just by trade publications but by mainstream media, probably because yes, he was quirky even by '60s standards, but also because he was such a refreshingly articulate and interesting thinker, with a charming and wry sense of humor—a man who made for a good, in-depth talk. In fact, Bowie's first interview, included here, which occurred in 1964 when he was still going by his given name David Jones, shows off his mature media savvy and wit perfectly, even though he was only sixteen at the time. It was his first public assumption

of a character: He convinced the BBC that he represented a
group of young men (in reality, his friends) who were feeling
persecuted by society because they had long hair. It was a gag,
but Bowie and his mates played it straight with their jovially
condescending interlocutor . . . And beyond the clever character pose, a truly hip public persona was born.

So hip, in fact, that Bowie deftly avoided becoming a
media fixture. Throughout the initial explosion of fame—the
Ziggy Stardust and Aladdin Sane years—he seemed to toe the
line perfectly between being available and not being available,
such that he was always a big "get" for a journalist, deserving
of cover treatment. Not that he was catty once he sat down to
talk, though. As shown in the two interviews from the early
1970s included here, he was nothing if not candid and open,
often self-critical, and always intelligent and witty. He had
a ready laugh and didn't hesitate to admit his working-class
background, to discuss his brother's mental-health issues, or,
for that matter, to risk criticism of important industry person-
ages—such as influential DJ John Peel. In short, he seemed to
have nothing to hide, and to be genuinely interested in speaking in depth to his audience.

Perhaps such thoughtful interviews were more work
than they seemed, or at least more deeply distracting, because
Bowie stopped giving interviews almost entirely for a spell
in the late 1970s during his sojourn in Berlin—when, by his
own standards, he made his favorite recordings. Those were
radically different recordings, with a sound not geared for pop
radio. What's more, by his own admission, he was trying to
quit drugs during that period. Whatever the reason, he let the
music speak for itself.

It wasn't long, though, before he resumed making himself accessible to the press again, particularly as he supported various new albums. But there's something about those interviews—such as Kurt Loder's insightful 1987 interview, or Bowie's look back at his film career in a *Movieline* chat, or his discussion with *Vox Pop* of the influence of John Lennon on his writing, all included here—that seem somehow wiser and sager, more contemplative, and reflective of a reputation to be confirmed or denied. Simply, he'd become a man who clearly felt it was incumbent upon him as an artist to be as open as he could be, even to such intense public scrutiny . . . yet felt it was also incumbent upon him to protect the mystery inherent in any art-making career.

All of which made for a rush of great interviews over the following decades. Bowie, ever the searcher, seemed to embrace the idea of the interview itself as an experimental form. This may be what led him, during this time, to a string of spirited interviews shared with other artists, or interviews of other artists conducted by Bowie himself. He'd shared the spotlight this way sporadically throughout his career—such as in Craig Copetas's marvelous 1974 interview for *Rolling Stone*, included here, of both Bowie and William Burroughs. But during the 1990s and into the 2000s, Bowie loved talking to other kinds of artists and drawing them out on pet subjects, as in his interviews here with fashion designer Alexander McQueen and visual artist Tracey Emin . . . or pet peeves, as in his talk with his own wife, supermodel Iman, wherein he explains his problems with feminism.

But the questing loquaciousness stopped abruptly in 2004 when Bowie had a heart attack—while onstage, no less, although he hid it and finished the show. After that, his biographers agree, he basically stopped giving not only performances but interviews as well. At least, in the way of traditional-format interviews.

Which is to say, his speaking interactions with the public after that became much more whimsical and offbeat. He published a list of 100 must-read books on his Facebook page. He provided novelist Rick Moody with a list of words he felt described one of his records.

And then there was the thing that was actually his last, sit-down-and-answer-questions interview: assuming yet another offbeat persona—a cocky yet insecure gag writer—Bowie went out the way he came in, with a gag interview with an offscreen Ricky Gervais, in a promotion for Gervais's television show, *Extras*, on which Bowie had appeared as a rather perverted version of himself.

Luckily, what Bowie didn't stop doing was making records—even releasing one, *Blackstar*, two days before his death. And interestingly, that record was a kind of self-interview—Bowie's most fearless and open of them all, wherein he answers the ultimate hard question "What is it like to be dying?"—and reveals in poetic detail what had meaning to him in his life . . . while addressing his audience with a certain innate gratitude as he says goodbye.

DAVID BOWIE

THE FIRST
INTERVIEW

INTERVIEW BY CLIFFORD MICHELMORE
BBC *TONIGHT*
NOVEMBER 1964

Cliff Michelmore interviews the spokesman for the Society for the Prevention of Cruelty to Long-Haired Men, David Bowie (then David Jones).

MICHELMORE: It's all got to stop! They've had enough! The worms are turning; the rebellion of the long hairs is getting underway. They're tired of persecution, they're tired of taunts, they're tired of losing their jobs, they're tired of being sent home from college, they're tired of being sent home from school, they're tired even of being refused the dole. So with a nucleus of, uh, some of his friends, a seventeen-year-old Davey Jones has just founded the Society for the Prevention of Cruelty to Long-Haired Men. Well, here we are. Long-Haired Men, you've got to have your hair, what, nine inches long before you can join?

BOWIE: Well, I think we've passed that over now.

MICHELMORE: Have you?

BOWIE: Yes.

MICHELMORE: Now, exactly who's been cruel to you?

BOWIE: Well, I think we're all fairly tolerant, but for the last two years we've heard, uh, comments like, "Darling!" and, "Can I carry your handbag?" thrown at us, and I think it just has to stop now.

MICHELMORE: But does it surprise you that you get this kind of comment? Because, after all, you've got really rather long hair, haven't you?

BOWIE: We have yes, yeah, it's not too bad, really . . . no, I like it, and I think we all like long hair, and, um, we don't see why other people should persecute us because of this.

MICHELMORE: How are you going to set about this campaign?

BOY NEXT TO BOWIE: Well, I don't know. I think the real sort of thing we should do is to try and get more followers behind us, so that we can sort of march in protest, sort of like ban the bomb all over again, you know, I mean, only against hair, people persecuting—

BOWIE: *Balder*-maston.*

---

* A pun on the Aldermaston marches, a series of protest marches held in London calling for the banning of nuclear weapons.

BOY NEXT TO BOWIE: [*Laughs*] —and I think gradually it will work, yeah, [*laughs*] yeah.

MICHELMORE: Oh, now you see a lot of people can't tell the difference between a man and a woman, can they? If you've got your hair *that* long.

BOY IN BACK ROW: No, well that's ridiculous, if the stage has got to the point when you can't tell either sex by a few inches of hair, I think it's pretty poor showing. Don't you?

MICHELMORE: Yeah, I do, yeah. Now, why did you grow your hair long in the first place?

SECOND BOY IN BACK ROW: Well, I think most of us just like it long where some like it short, um, others like us like it long. It's nice—

MICHELMORE: But, but did you grow it long at all to stand out in a crowd?

THIRD BOY IN BACK ROW: Mine was an accident. I just forgot to have it cut for quite some time.

MULTIPLE VOICES: No, no.

MICHELMORE: Yeah, for a long time, I should think. [*Laughter*] Well, well, well, I mean, did you, did you get this off the Rolling Stones, really?

MULTIPLE VOICES: Oh no, no, definitely not.

BOWIE: That's, that's stupid.

MICHELMORE: But did any of you have your hair growing long more than two years ago or so?

MULTIPLE VOICES: Oh, yeah, yes.

MICHELMORE: Did you? Before the Rolling Stones ever did.

BOWIE: Well, it takes a long time to get this length, you know.

OFF-CAMERA VOICE: It just doesn't grow overnight, just because the Rolling Stones did it.

OFF-CAMERA VOICE: [*Overlapping*] It's quite easy to, uh, cut them out.

MICHELMORE: Can, can I ask you what you say when you're going to the hairdresser's. When are you going to the hairdresser's?

MULTIPLE VOICES: We don't, we don't go.

BOY TO FAR RIGHT: Mine was last year. [*Laughter*]

MICHELMORE: Don't you go and have it shampooed and set?

MULTIPLE VOICES: Oh no, no.

BOWIE: Our Mums do it, if anything. [*Laughter*]

MICHELMORE: Your mothers do it?

BOWIE: Yeah! Why shouldn't they?

MICHELMORE: Do they?

BOWIE: Yeah, very good at it, better than I could ever be.

MICHELMORE: When, when was the last time that any of you ever went to a barber's?

BOWIE: Three years ago.

MICHELMORE: Three years.

OFF-CAMERA VOICE: I went just over a year ago.

STANDING BOY ON FAR RIGHT: I only did because I had an operation. [*Laughter*]

MICHELMORE: Exactly how are you going to stop people being cruel to you? [*Points to* **BOWIE**] Come on now, it's your idea.

BOWIE: Well, if anybody is chucked out of a factory job or, uh, removed from a public bar, saloon bar, um, we'll get a petition written up and sent to the, either the LCC, the people that hold the pub and its license, or—

MICHELMORE: But do you think this will do any good?

BOWIE: Well, it better do good. [*All laugh*]

OFF-CAMERA VOICE: It will help, people will eventually I think come, uh, sort of—

MICHELMORE: But do you really think that many people are on your side, is what I'm saying?

BOWIE: Oh, yes.

MULTIPLE VOICES: Quite a few. Quite a lot.

BOWIE: A thousand teenagers over Britain.

MICHELMORE: All of them with long hair?

OFF-CAMERA VOICE: No. Lots of them would *like* to have long hair.

BOWIE: No, not lots of them. They haven't got permission

BLONDE FROM PREVIOUS COMMENTS: They're just wishing they had got long hair.

BOY WITH SCARF: Either their, uh, company they work with or their parents don't allow them to have long hair, maybe.

MICHELMORE: No, well, I, I well understand this, can't you. Mind you, I'm talking out of a sort of sense of, um, jealousy, in a way, seeing you over there with so much, and I should've gone and had a haircut today. [*Laughter*]

DAVID BOWIE TELLS ALL AND MORE

INTERVIEW BY PATRICK SALVO
INTERVIEW
MARCH 1973

SALVO: You were born in Brixton, how far were you from Her Majesty's Prison?

BOWIE: About 700 yards.

SALVO: You had a good view, then.

BOWIE: They had a good view of me as well.

SALVO: What does imprisonment mean to you?

BOWIE: I think I've been in prison for the last 24 years. I think coming to America has opened one door.

SALVO: Do you ever get imprisoned by your writings?

BOWIE: No—I never get trapped by them. I lose them. They divorce me. Once I've written something it does tend to run away from me. I don't seem to have any part of it—it's no longer my piece of writing.

SALVO: Do you write to gain or lose your identity?

BOWIE: Possibly to understand it. I don't think either to lose or gain.

SALVO: It seems as even you once said, "You say most things the long way 'round."

BOWIE: I do tend to. I'm not very articulate.

SALVO: Your songs tingle of extreme difficulties and social diseases, yet is there any definite solution to these problems in your works?

BOWIE: I suppose it stems from a non-understanding of the problems I was faced with. I used parody as a form of defense. Most people attack it that way.

SALVO: Can you give us some background?

BOWIE: Sure. I was born in London 1947, after the war. A real wartime baby. I went to school in Brixton and then I moved up to Yorkshire, which is in the north of England. I lived on the farms up there. So I've seen pretty well the best of both from the terrible slum area of Brixton, with a pretty heavy black population, to right up in the country on the farms. I've been a child through both so that both halves of it really influenced me and produced a schizoid attitude in life. I think that's what confused me, because having seen the best of both I couldn't cope with a lot of problems that were around. Now that I've come to America a lot of those problems have become very graphic. In fact, I just called up my wife and told her that I'd like to settle here for a year or two. A lot of things have opened up in the last three days. It's really changed me around, it really has. There's a lot of fabulous people here. Their views are so heavy, so pointed that it becomes very well analyzed, what is going on in this country. My country is in the depths of lethargy and very apathetic, there is very little happening. There's no action in my country. This is quite a challenge to come over to a country like this where for me the most important thing to me is that the music is a communicative blanket media. Where at home it's merely something to listen to.

SALVO: It's a way of life here for people where in Great Britain it's more or less taken for granted.

BOWIE: Very much so. It's nice, so it sells well, the people enjoy it purely as music. Over here . . .

SALVO: It's almost like a religion.

BOWIE: No, I wouldn't say that. I'd say it's the most honest media that you have over here. Whether it's a bit late because of the process of making a record and reproducing it. Whether it's late or not doesn't matter because it's honest and anything honest when it comes out means something.

SALVO: What do you think of the media in Great Britain?

BOWIE: I think it's better than yours, I think better use is made of it, although it's terribly biased to the left.

SALVO: How about your radio format?

BOWIE: Radio in England is nonexistent. It's very bad English use of a media system, typically English use.

SALVO: Even people who do get a chance to play some decent music only have limited airtime. For instance, John Peel.

BOWIE: There's the *John Peel Show* and there is *Sound of the Seventies* and that's it. I also believe there's a concert now—a live concert for an hour. But there's a good television program called *Disco 2*. It's quite good but again it's average, average. It's all on a down play. You know we've got this thing in England to be hip is to speak very down—like John Peel. And that just about sums up England. They don't realize when they talk like that, then that is what they represent—absolutely. John underplaying everything like vodka. Totally kind of frustrating within himself I suppose.

SALVO: He's doing an awful lot but he's doing nothing.

BOWIE: Yeah—promoting a non-image.

SALVO: Are you content existing in the form of a human—it seems like you're down on most of the human race but you're rather personal in your writings.

BOWIE: Especially now, especially now this is true you don't know how important this trip has been, I just did Europe but the climate in Europe is completely divorced from what's happening over here. It's a different world. Everything is in a different perspective now. Absolutely.

SALVO: I remember you saying once that you've already had most of the experiences that you're likely to go through in the next forty years.

BOWIE: I feel so—I feel so.

SALVO: You were through the experiences perhaps, but . . .

BOWIE: Yeah—I went through a lot of experiences. I've been through a lot as a boy, as a teenager, and I'm still going through them now and there is no stop.

SALVO: This "growing up before one's time" can at times lead to any amount of various functional disorders.

BOWIE: Yes, it does do.

SALVO: This is found quite plainly in some of your writings.

BOWIE: Yes, you're right. It happened to my brother. Do you know the new album?

SALVO: *The Man Who Sold the World.*

BOWIE: There's a track on that based on my brother, called "All the Madmen."

SALVO: I heard he was in the hospital.

BOWIE: Yeah—in fact I just phoned up my wife and it seems he's staying with us now. She wouldn't tell me on the phone because he was in the room. I'm not sure whether he kinda ran away or what. He's only twenty-eight, maybe thirty. But, I mean, there's a schizoid streak within the family anyway so I dare say that I'm affected by that. The majority of the people in my family have been in some kind of mental institution. As for my brother he doesn't want to leave. He likes it very much. He's just been changed to a new one, but the old one, Cain Hill, he really dug. He'd be happy to spend the rest of his life there—mainly because most of the people are on the same wavelength as him. And he's not a freak, he's a very straight person.

SALVO: Did he walk in on his own two feet?

BOWIE: My mother signed him in, which is very sad, but she's been in as well. She thought it did her good but it didn't. We had to take her on holiday, we put her out in Cyprus for a bit. It's getting very starchy. Ah! The time element you were speaking of. Listen, I want to lay a concept on you. Do you know a guy by the name of George Meyer, he runs the Walrus? He's just read the Marshall McLuhan book *From Cliché to Archetype*, he tried to explain it to me the best way he could and this is where I lost my mind: whatever the present pop art form may be, it is already clichéd. It's typesetted whether it's put down by the critics and artists as being superfurious non-being, for example Charlie Chaplin, Buster Keaton films, those people. At the time, they were written in the morning, shot in the evening and they'd make a lot of bread and everybody thought they were quite funny, right? Now Charlie Chaplin has an academic following and he is now a genius. The rock & rock revival, the same thing. They've brought it out now and dusted it off, beautified. Example, Creedence Clearwater.

SALVO: What rock & roll revival?

BOWIE: Just the general feeling that rock & roll is/was good. All of it you know—like anything, they'd take out some trite and play it. At the time you thought it was a novelty record. After two plays you got good and fed up with it. And now they play it and it's marveled as spectacular, really great.

SALVO: Because of the nostalgia involved.

BOWIE: And the '30s and '40s and so on. Now here's the crunch. So an astronaut goes to the moon, takes a photograph of the earth, comes back and sets up an Archetypal Earth which is no longer useful. It's now in the past. People are cleaning it up—ecology and so on. So where are we now? What's the next step after that one? Boy that's a heavy theory. Nobody in England would get that—I mean it doesn't mean anything up there. They're still convinced that there's a revolution. They're so disillusioned. That's why I haven't been

getting into it anymore. I have to stay with my own circle of
friends, my wife . . .

SALVO: Are most of your friends artists, performers, and the
like?

BOWIE: No musical friends except Marc Bolan from T-Rex is
the only friend I have in the business. Do you have Jehovah's
Witnesses over here?

SALVO: Sure, they used to visit my mother quite often, but I
think she was putting them all on. They wouldn't say no, but
she wouldn't say no either so it was a gas. As for yourself, you
obviously don't believe in organized religion but you were
once a Buddhist. You practiced it and that would be organized to an extent.

BOWIE: Well that's why I'm not a Buddhist anymore. I wrote
a song called "The Supermen" which was about the Homo
Superior race and through that I got interested in Nazism.
I'm overwhelmed at their methods—diabolical. I have no
room in my head to entertain their theory, the gross effects,
the terrible disregard for human life, especially for particular
races and religions. You knew Roman Catholics were next.
The Pope bought Hitler off. It was the whole thing about
the Magic Wine. Hitler wanted to develop an Aryan race.
For what reason? To fight Homo Superior. He was dread-
fully afraid of Homo Superior and his aims to develop a race
of Aryan people was a misrepresentation of that good feeling of Homo Superior. Because it was such a depressed era,

spiritually and morally, that it came out all wrong. I'm sure Hitler could have gone the other way. But mind you this is a mad planet, it's doomed to madness. We might have freaked the world so much, twisted it off its axis, its practical and mental axis so much that the way these new children could be influenced by their grandparents might have ticked something off in their head that you may well find that we have given birth to Homo Superior prematurely.

SALVO: In another one your songs, "Cygnet Committee," you get totally involved in the so-called militant hippie movement.

BOWIE: Wow—why did you pick that one? That's crazy, nobody picks that one, they get hung up on "Memory of a Free Festival," "Space Oddity," and that's it. Maybe "Janine," but this is remarkable.

SALVO: It's rather long and involved and it is in segments, isn't it?

BOWIE: I basically wanted it to be a cry to fucking humanity. The beginning of the song when I first started it was saying—Fellow man I do love you—I love humanity, I adore it, it's sensational, sensuous, exciting—it sparkled and it's also pathetic at the same time. And it was a cry to list O.K., that was the first section. And then I tried to get into the dialogue between two kinds of forces. First the sponsor of the revolution, the quasi-capitalist who believes that he is left wing and puts support into a lot of the pure—what ended up being what I anticipated [from] that particular movement for quite a few months over in England. People like Mick Farren, Jerry Rubin, etc.

SALVO: Mick Farren, formerly a deviant and a Pink Fairy, now leader of the British White Panthers.

BOWIE: And that's what I saw coming up.

SALVO: Do you think they had a valid thing?

BOWIE: Rubin, no not at all, it's set up so many false values, so many bad standards, such intolerance and hypocrisy. I mean the truest form of any form of revolutionary left, whatever you want to call it was Jack Kerouac, e. e. cummings, and Ginsberg's period. Excuse me, but that's where it was at. The hippies, I'm afraid, don't know what's happening. I don't think there are any anyway. The underground really went underground. Grand Funk, and all these people man are the moderate's choice of music. Underground is Yoko Ono, the Black Poets. These people scare the hell out of most freaks. They laugh at Yoko Ono, but it's the whole cliché.

SALVO: It's like when Lennon makes a movie and everybody is told to disrobe, the cat who runs around fully clothed is the most obscene.

BOWIE: Right, John Lennon comes in the same period. He was into Ginsberg before he was into anything else.

SALVO: So do you think there really is or was a movement?

BOWIE: There was a movement, but the revolution has been fought on an entirely different plane to the plane that I thought it should be fought on. It was intrinsically bad. Every time there was something to say, for any and every form of people's society. For instance, like capitalism can be all right, I mean Marx didn't live to see what Roosevelt did with that depression. He pulled everybody out of that depressed and everybody hated Roosevelt. He got into office four times. One after the other, with everybody saying, he can't get in again. Everybody voted for Roosevelt four times and he did a hell of a lot. Mind you, I'm a little political, not too much but I'm branching off very much here. You see I'm just getting quick flashes of what I think.

SALVO: Then it goes on:

> Infiltrated business cesspools
> Hating through our sleeves,
> Yea, and we slit the Catholic throat
> "Wish You Could Hear"
> "Love Is All We Need"
> "Kick Out The Jams"
> "Kick Out Your Mother"
> "Cut Up Your Friend"
> "Screw Up Your Brother or He'll Get You in the End."

BOWIE: Sure, all the clichés, passé stuff—again, parody.

SALVO: At the very finale you state that you want to believe. At times this is quite difficult, but exactly in what do you want to believe in?

BOWIE: I would like to believe that people knew what they were fighting for and why they wanted a revolution, and exactly what it was within that they didn't like. I mean, to put down a society or the aims of a society is to put down a hell of a lot of people and that scares me that there should be such a division where one set of people are saying that another set should be killed. You know you can't put down anybody. You can just try and understand. The emphasis shouldn't be on revolution, it should be on communication. Because it's just going to get more uptight. The more the revolution goes on, there will be a civil war sooner or later.

SALVO: Over here there's one every summer. Finally, would you care to elaborate on the state of the English youth today?

BOWIE: I wouldn't care to.

SALVO: It's that bad?

BOWIE: It's not that bad, but it's so crazy.

SALVO: Do you think it will come together in the end, will they suss it out somehow?

BOWIE: I don't think there's any chance of sussing it out. I think there will be a period where man will be fairly content. More content than he's been for some time. Since early middle ages when people were generally taking away the barbarity of their life, were pretty content. Although it was all an illicit contentment, what with the slave systems all over the world, in England especially, the peasants and the master, etc. People were incredibly content. There will be another age of contentment. I don't know how long.

SALVO: This is the age of apathy in Great Britain mainly because they really don't have much to commit themselves to. It would be different if England were totally involved in a war . . .

BOWIE: Exactly, exactly they want to be Americanized, a lot of them are hippies and they're so shook up man 'cause they've got nothing to fight and that makes them so frustrated.

SALVO: They're given the vote at eighteen, you know, sign contracts—big deal.

BOWIE: There's nothing to vote for anyway and nothing's really bad enough to bother to replace it, 'cause you can get through.

SALVO: They're frustrated because they really don't have a valid grievance to revolt against but they all got two legs.

BOWIE: That's why they switch from one subject to another in

England all the time. One moment it's Black Power, the next moment it's the war in Vietnam—anything just to grab onto until it gets a bit boring because nothing actually happens. It's like THIS SKETCH IS A BIT SILLY, LET'S GO ON TO THE NEXT ONE.

BEAT GODFATHER MEETS GLITTER MAINMAN

WILLIAM BURROUGHS, SAY HELLO TO DAVID BOWIE

INTERVIEW BY CRAIG COPETAS
ROLLING STONE
FEBRUARY 28, 1974

William Seward Burroughs is not a talkative man. Once at a dinner he gazed down into a pair of stereo microphones trained to pick up his every munch and said, "I don't like talk and I don't like talkers. Like Ma Barker. You remember Ma Barker? Well, that's what she always said, 'Ma Barker doesn't like talk and she doesn't like talkers.' She just sat there with her gun."

This was on my mind as much as the mysterious personality of David Bowie when an Irish cabbie drove Burroughs and me to Bowie's London home on November 17th ("Strange blokes down this part o' London, mate"). I had spent the last several weeks arranging this two-way interview. I had brought Bowie all of Burroughs's novels: *Naked Lunch*, *Nova Express*, *The Ticket That Exploded*, and the rest. He'd only had time to read *Nova Express*. Burroughs for his part had only heard two Bowie songs, "Five Years" and "Star Man," though he had read all of Bowie's lyrics. Still they had expressed interest in meeting each other.

Bowie's house is decorated in a science-fiction mode: A gigantic painting, by an artist whose style fell midway between Salvador Dali and Norman Rockwell, hangs over a plastic sofa. Quite a contrast to Burroughs's humble two-room Piccadilly flat, decorated with photos of Brion Gysin—modest quarters for such a successful writer, more like the Beat Hotel in Paris than anything else.

Soon Bowie entered, wearing three-tone NASA jodhpurs. He jumped right into a detailed description of the painting and its surrealistic qualities. Burroughs nodded, and the interview/conversation began. The three of us sat in the room for two hours, talking and taking lunch: a Jamaican fish dish, prepared by a Jamaican in the Bowie entourage, with avocados stuffed with shrimp and a beaujolais nouveau, served by two interstellar Bowieites.

There was immediate liking and respect between the two. In fact, a few days after the conversation, Bowie asked Burroughs for a favor: A production of *The Maids* staged by Lindsey Kemp, Bowie's old mime teacher, had been closed down in London by playwright Jean Genet's London publisher. Bowie wanted to bring the matter to Genet's attention personally. Burroughs was impressed by Bowie's description of the production and promised to help. A few weeks later Bowie went to Paris in search of Genet, following leads from Burroughs.

Who knows? Perhaps a collaboration has begun; perhaps, as Bowie says, they may be the Rogers and Hammerstein of the Seventies.

• • •

BURROUGHS: Do you do all your designs yourself?

BOWIE: Yes, I have to take total control myself. I can't let anybody else do anything, for I find that I can do things better for me. I don't want to get other people playing with what they think that I'm trying to do. I don't like to read things that people write about me. I'd rather read what kids have to say about me, because it's not their profession to do that.

People look to me to see what the spirit of the Seventies is, at least 50 percent of them do. Critics I don't understand. They get too intellectual. They're not very well versed in street talk; it takes them longer to say it. So they have to do it in dictionaries and they take longer to say it.

I went to a middle-class school, but my background is working class. I got the best of both worlds, I saw both classes, so I have a pretty fair idea of how people live and why they do it. I can't articulate it too well, but I have a feeling about it. But not the upper class. I want to meet the Queen and then I'll know. How do you take the picture that people paint of you?

BURROUGHS: They try to categorize you. They want to see their picture of you and if they don't see their picture of you they're very upset. Writing is seeing how close you can come to make it happen, that's the object of all art. What else do they think man really wants, a whiskey priest on a mission he doesn't believe in? I think the most important thing in the world is that the artists should take over this planet because they're the only ones who can make anything happen. Why should we let these fucking newspaper politicians take over from us?

BOWIE: I change my mind a lot. I usually don't agree with what I say very much. I'm an awful liar.

BURROUGHS: I am too.

BOWIE: I'm not sure whether it is me changing my mind, or whether I lie a lot. It's somewhere between the two. I don't exactly lie, I change my mind all the time. People are always throwing things at me that I've said and I say that I didn't mean anything. You can't stand still on one point for your entire life.

BURROUGHS: Only politicians lay down what they think and that is it. Take a man like Hitler, he never changed his mind.

BOWIE: *Nova Express* really reminded me of *Ziggy Stardust,* which I am going to be putting into a theatrical performance. Forty scenes are in it and it would be nice if the characters and actors learned the scenes and we all shuffled them around in a hat the afternoon of the performance and just performed it as the scenes come out. I got this all from you, Bill . . . so it would change every night.

BURROUGHS: That's a very good idea, visual cut-up in a different sequence.

BOWIE: I get bored very quickly and that would give it some new energy. I'm rather kind of old school, thinking that when an artist does his work it's no longer his . . . I just see what people make of it. That is why the TV production of *Ziggy* will have to exceed people's expectations of what they thought *Ziggy* was.

BURROUGHS: Could you explain this Ziggy Stardust image of yours? From what I can see it has to do with the world being on the eve of destruction within five years.

BOWIE: The time is five years to go before the end of the earth. It has been announced that the world will end because of lack of natural resources. [The album was released three years ago.] Ziggy is in a position where all the kids have access to things that they thought they wanted. The older people have lost all touch with reality and the kids are left on their own to plunder anything. Ziggy was in a rock & roll band and the kids no longer want rock & roll. There's no electricity to play it. Ziggy's adviser tells him to collect news and sing it, 'cause there is no news. So Ziggy does this and there is terrible news. "All the Young Dudes" is a song about this news. It is no hymn to the youth as people thought. It is completely the opposite.

BURROUGHS: Where did this Ziggy idea come from, and this five-year idea? Of course, exhaustion of natural resources will not develop the end of the world. It will result in the collapse of civilization. And it will cut down the population by about three quarters.

BOWIE: Exactly. This does not cause the end of the world for Ziggy. The end comes when the infinites arrive. They really are a black hole, but I've made them people because it would be very hard to explain a black hole onstage.

BURROUGHS: Yes, a black hole onstage would be an incredible expense. And it would be a continuing performance, first eating up Shaftesbury Avenue.

BOWIE: Ziggy is advised in a dream by the infinites to write the coming of a starman, so he writes "Starman," which is the first news of hope that the people have heard. So they latch onto it immediately. The starmen that he is talking about are called the infinites, and they are black-hole jumpers. Ziggy has been talking about this amazing spaceman who will be coming down to save the earth. They arrive somewhere in Greenwich Village. They don't have a care in the world and are of no possible use to us. They just happened to stumble into our universe by black-hole jumping. Their whole life is traveling from universe to universe. In the stage show, one of them resembles Brando, another one is a black New Yorker. I even have one called Queenie the Infinite Fox.

Now Ziggy starts to believe in all this himself and thinks himself a prophet of the future starman. He takes himself up to incredible spiritual heights and is kept alive by his disciples. When the infinites arrive, they take bits of Ziggy to make themselves real because in their original state they are anti-matter and cannot exist on our world. And they tear him to pieces onstage during the song "Rock 'n' Roll Suicide." As soon as Ziggy dies onstage the infinites take his elements and make themselves visible. It is a science-fiction fantasy of today and this is what literally blew my head off when I read *Nova Express*, which was written in 1961. Maybe we are the Rogers and Hammerstein of the Seventies, Bill!

BURROUGHS: Yes, I can believe that. The parallels are definitely there, and it sounds good.

BOWIE: I must have the total image of a stage show. It has to be total with me. I'm just not content writing songs, I want to make it three-dimensional. Songwriting as an art is a bit archaic now. Just writing a song is not good enough.

BURROUGHS: It's the whole performance. It's not like somebody sitting down at the piano and just playing a piece.

BOWIE: A song has to take on character, shape, body, and influence people to an extent that they use it for their own devices. It must affect them not just as a song, but as a lifestyle. The rock stars have assimilated all kinds of philosophies, styles, histories, writings, and they throw out what they have gleaned from that.

BURROUGHS: The revolution will come from ignoring the others out of existence.

BOWIE: Really. Now we have people who are making it happen on a level faster than ever. People who are into groups like Alice Cooper, the New York Dolls, and Iggy Pop, who are denying totally and irrevocably the existence of people who are into the Stones and the Beatles. The gap has decreased from twenty years to ten years.

BURROUGHS: The escalating rate of change. The media are really responsible for most of this. Which produces an incalculable effect.

BOWIE: Once upon a time, even when I was thirteen or four-teen, for me it was between fourteen and forty that you were old. Basically. But now it is eighteen-year-olds and twenty-six-year-olds—there can be incredible discrepancies, which is really quite alarming. We are not trying to bring people to-gether, but to wonder how much longer we've got. It would be positively boring if minds were in tune. I'm more inter-ested in whether the planet is going to survive.

BURROUGHS: Actually, the contrary is happening; people are getting further and further apart.

BOWIE: The idea of getting minds together smacks of the Flower Power period to me. The coming together of people I find obscene as a principle. It is not human. It is not a natural thing as some people would have us believe.

COPETAS: What about love?

BURROUGHS: Ugh.

BOWIE: I'm not at ease with the word "love."

BURROUGHS: I'm not either.

BOWIE: I was told that it was cool to fall in love, and that period was nothing like that to me. I gave too much of my time and energy to another person and they did the same to me and we started burning out against each other. And that is what is termed love . . . that we decide to put all our values on another person. It's like two pedestals, each wanting to be the other pedestal.

BURROUGHS: I don't think that "love" is a useful word. It is predicated on a separation of a thing called sex and a thing called love and that they are separate. Like the primitive expressions in the old South when the woman is on a pedestal, and the man worshipped his wife and then went out and fucked a whore. It is primarily a Western concept and then it extended to the whole Flower Power thing of loving everybody. Well, you can't do that because the interests are not the same.

BOWIE: The word is wrong, I'm sure. It is the way you understand love. The love that you see, among people who say, "We're in love," it's nice to look at . . . but wanting not to be alone, wanting to have a person there that they relate to for a few years is not often the love that carries on throughout the lives of those people. There is another word. I'm not sure whether it is a word. Love is every type of relationship that you think of . . . I'm sure it means relationship, every type of relationship that you can think of.

COPETAS: What of sexuality, where is it going?

BOWIE: Sexuality and where it is going is an extraordinary question, for I don't see it going anywhere. It is with me, and that's it. It's not coming out as a new advertising campaign next year. It's just there. Everything you can think about sexuality is just there. Maybe there are different kinds of sexuality, maybe they'll be brought into play more. Like one time it was impossible to be homosexual as far as the public were concerned. Now it is accepted. Sexuality will never change, for people have been fucking their own particular ways since time began and will continue to do it. Just more of those ways will be coming to light. It might even reach a puritan state.

BURROUGHS: There are certain indications that it might be going that way in the future, real backlash.

BOWIE: Oh yes, look at the rock business. Poor old Clive Davis. He was found to be absconding with money and there were also drug things tied up with it. And that has started a whole clean-up campaign among record companies; they're starting to ditch some of their artists.

I'm regarded quite asexually by a lot of people. And the people that understand me the best are nearer to what I understand about me. Which is not very much, for I'm still searching. I don't know, the people who are coming anywhere close to where I think I'm at regard me more as an erogenous kind of thing. But the people who don't know so much about me regard me more sexually.

But there again, maybe it's the disinterest with sex after a certain age, because the people who do kind of get nearer to me are generally older. And the ones who regard me as more of a sexual thing are generally younger. The younger people get into the lyrics in a different way; there's much more of a tactile understanding, which is the way I prefer it. 'Cause that's the way I get off on writing, especially William's. I can't say that I analyze it all and that's exactly what you're saying, but from a feeling way I got what you meant. It's there, a whole wonderhouse of strange shapes and colors, tastes, feelings.

I must confess that up until now I haven't been an avid reader of William's work. I really did not get past Kerouac to be honest. But when I started looking at your work I really couldn't believe it. Especially after reading *Nova Express*. I really related to that. My ego obviously put me on to the "Pay Color" chapter, then I started dragging out lines from the rest of the book.

BURROUGHS: Your lyrics are quite perceptive.

BOWIE: They're a bit middle class, but that's all right, 'cause I'm middle class.

BURROUGHS: It is rather surprising that they are such complicated lyrics, that can go down with a mass audience. The content of most pop lyrics is practically zero, like "Power to the People."

BOWIE: I'm quite certain that the audience that I've got for my stuff don't listen to the lyrics.

BURROUGHS: That's what I'm interested in hearing about . . . do they understand them?

BOWIE: Well, it comes over more as a media thing and it's only after they sit down and bother to look. On what level they are reading them, they do understand them, because they will send me back their own kind of write-ups of what

I'm talking about, which is great for me because sometimes I don't know. There have been times when I've written something and it goes out and it comes back in a letter from some kid as to what they think about it and I've taken their analysis to heart so much that I have taken up his thing. Writing what my audience is telling me to write.

Lou Reed is the most important definitive writer in modern rock. Not because of the stuff that he does, but the direction that he will take it. Half the new bands would not be around if it were not for Lou. The movement that Lou's stuff has created is amazing. New York City is Lou Reed. Lou writes in the street-gut level and the English tend to intellectualize more.

BURROUGHS: What is your inspiration for writing, is it literary?

BOWIE: I don't think so.

BURROUGHS: Well, I read this eight-line poem of yours and it is very reminiscent of T. S. Eliot.

BOWIE: Never read him.

BURROUGHS: [*Laughs*] It is very reminiscent of "Waste Land." Do you get any of your ideas from dreams?

BOWIE: Frequently.

BURROUGHS: I get 70 percent of mine from dreams.

BOWIE: There's a thing that just as you go to sleep, if you keep your elbows elevated that you will never go below the dream stage. And I've used that quite a lot and it keeps me dreaming much longer than if I just relaxed.

BURROUGHS: I dream a great deal, and then because I am a light sleeper, I will wake up and jot down just a few words and they will always bring the whole idea back to me.

BOWIE: I keep a tape recorder by the bed and then if anything comes I just say it into the tape recorder. As for my inspiration, I haven't changed my views much since I was about twelve, really, I've just got a twelve-year-old mentality. When I was in school I had a brother who was into Kerouac and he gave me *On the Road* to read when I was twelve years old. That's still been a big influence.

COPETAS: The images both of you transpire are very graphic, almost comic-booky in nature.

BOWIE: Well, yes, I find it easier to write in these little vignettes; if I try to get any more heavy, I find myself out of my league. I couldn't contain myself in what I say. Besides if you are really heavier there isn't that much more time to read that much, or listen to that much. There's not much point in getting any heavier . . . there's too many things to read and look at. If people read three hours of what you've done, then they'll analyze it for seven hours and come out with seven hours of their own thinking . . . where if you give them thirty seconds of your own stuff they usually still come out with seven hours of their own thinking. They take hook images of what you do. And they pontificate on the hooks. The sense of the immediacy of the image. Things have to hit for the moment. That's one of the reasons I'm into video; the image has to hit immediately. I adore video and the whole cutting up of it.

What are your projects at the moment?

BURROUGHS: At the moment I'm trying to set up an institute of advanced studies somewhere in Scotland. Its aim will be to extend awareness and alter consciousness in the direction of greater range, flexibility, and effectiveness at a time when traditional disciplines have failed to come up with viable solutions. You see, the advent of the space age and the possibility of exploring galaxies and contacting alien life forms poses an urgent necessity for radically new solutions. We will be considering only non-chemical methods with the emphasis placed on combination, synthesis, interaction, and rotation of methods now being used in the East and West, together with methods that are not at present being used to extend awareness or increase human potentials.

We know exactly what we intend to do and how to go about doing it. As I said, no drug experiments are planned and no drugs other than alcohol, tobacco, and personal medications obtained on prescription will be permitted in the center. Basically, the experiments we propose are inexpensive and easy to carry out. Things such as yoga-style meditation and exercises, communication, sound, light and film experiments, experiments with sensory deprivation chambers, pyramids, psychotronic generators and Reich's orgone accumulators, experiments with infra-sound, experiments with dream and sleep.

BOWIE: That sounds fascinating. Are you basically interested in energy forces?

BURROUGHS: Expansion of awareness, eventually leading to mutations. Did you read *Journey Out of the Body*? Not the usual book on astral projection. This American businessman found he was having these experiences of getting out of the body—never used any hallucinogenic drugs. He's now setting up this astral air force. This psychic thing is really a rave in the States now. Did you experience it much when you were there?

BOWIE: No, I really hid from it purposely. I was studying Tibetan Buddhism when I was quite young, again influenced by Kerouac. The Tibetan Buddhist Institute was available so I trotted down there to have a look. Lo and behold there's a guy down in the basement who's the head man in setting up a place in Scotland for the refugees, and I got involved purely on a sociological level—because I wanted to help get the refugees out of India, for they were really having a shitty time of it down there, dropping like flies due to the change of atmosphere from the Himalayas.

Scotland was a pretty good place to put them, and then more and more I was drawn to their way of thinking, or non thinking, and for a while got quite heavily involved in it. I got to the point where I wanted to become a novice monk and about two weeks before I was actually going to take those steps, I broke up and went out on the streets and got drunk and never looked back.

BURROUGHS: Just like Kerouac.

BOWIE: Go to the States much?

BURROUGHS: Not since '71.

BOWIE: It has changed, I can tell you, since then.

BURROUGHS: When were you last back?

BOWIE: About a year ago.

BURROUGHS: Did you see any of the porn films in New York?

BOWIE: Yes, quite a few.

BURROUGHS: When I was last back, I saw about thirty of them. I was going to be a judge at the erotic film festival.

BOWIE: The best ones were the German ones; they were really incredible.

BURROUGHS: I thought that the American ones were still the best. I really like film . . . I understand that you may play Valentine Michael Smith in the film version of *Stranger in a Strange Land.*

BOWIE: No, I don't like the book much. In fact, I think it is terrible. It was suggested to me that I make it into a movie, then I got around to reading it. It seemed a bit too Flower-Powery and that made me a bit wary.

BURROUGHS: I'm not that happy with the book either. You know, science fiction has not been very successful. It was supposed to start a whole new trend and nothing happened. For the special effects in some of the movies, like *2001*, it was great. But it all ended there.

BOWIE: I feel the same way. Now I'm doing Orwell's *1984* on television; that's a political thesis and an impression of the way of another country. Something of that nature will have more impact on television. I don't believe in proper cinema; it doesn't have the strength of television. People having to go out to the cinema is really archaic. I'd much rather sit at home.

BURROUGHS: Do you mean the whole concept of the audience?

BOWIE: Yes, it is ancient. No sense of immediacy.

BURROUGHS: Exactly, it all relates back to image and the way in which it is used.

BOWIE: Right. I'd like to start a TV station.

BURROUGHS: There are hardly any programs worth anything any more. The British TV is a little better than American. The best thing the British do is natural history. There was one last week with sea lions eating penguins, incredible. There is no reason for dull programs, people get very bored with housing projects and coal strikes.

BOWIE: They all have an interest level of about three seconds. Enough time to get into the commentator's next sentence. And that is the premise it works on. I'm going to put together all the bands that I think are of great value in the States and England, then make an hour-long program about them. Probably a majority of people have never heard of these bands. They are doing and saying things in a way other bands aren't. Things like the Puerto Rican music at the Cheetah Club in New York. I want people to hear musicians like Joe Cuba. He has done things to whole masses of Puerto Rican people. The music is fantastic and important. I also want to start getting Andy Warhol films on TV.

BURROUGHS: Have you ever met Warhol?

BOWIE: Yes, about two years ago I was invited up to The Factory. We got in the lift and went up and when it opened there was a brick wall in front of us. We rapped on the wall and they didn't believe who we were. So we went back down and back up again till finally they opened the wall and everybody was peering around at each other. That was shortly after the gun incident. I met this man who was the living dead. Yellow in complexion, a wig on that was the wrong color, little glasses. I extended my hand and the guy retired, so I thought, "The guy doesn't like flesh, obviously he's reptilian." He produced a camera and took a picture of me. And I tried to make small talk with him, and it wasn't getting anywhere.

But then he saw my shoes. I was wearing a pair of gold-and-yellow shoes, and he says, "I adore those shoes, tell me where you got those shoes." He then started a whole rap about shoe design and that broke the ice. My yellow shoes broke the ice with Andy Warhol.

I adore what he was doing. I think his importance was very heavy, it's become a big thing to like him now. But Warhol wanted to be cliché, he wanted to be available in Woolworth's, and be talked about in that glib type of manner. I hear he wants to make real films now, which is very sad because the films he was making were the things that should be happening. I left knowing as little about him as a person as when I went in.

BURROUGHS: I don't think that there is any person there. It's a very alien thing, completely and totally unemotional. He's really a science-fiction character. He's got a strange green color.

BOWIE: That's what struck me. He's the wrong color, this man is the wrong color to be a human being. Especially under the stark neon lighting that is in The Factory. Apparently it is a real experience to behold him in the daylight.

BURROUGHS: I've seen him in all light and still have no idea as to what is going on, except that it is something quite purposeful. It's not energetic, but quite insidious, completely asexual. His films will be the late-night movies of the future.

BOWIE: Exactly. Remember *Pork*? I want to get that onto TV. TV has eaten up everything else, and Warhol films are all that are left, which is fabulous. *Pork* could become the next *I Love*

Lucy, the great American domestic comedy. It's about how people really live, not like Lucy, who never touched dishwater. It's about people living and hustling to survive.

That's what *Pork* is all about. A smashing of the spectacle. Although I'd like to do my own version of *Sinbad the Sailor*. I think that is an all-time classic. But it would have to be done on an extraordinary level. It would be incredibly indulgent and expensive. It would have to utilize lasers and all the things that are going to happen in a true fantasy.

Even the use of holograms. Holograms are important. Videotape is next, then it will be holograms. Holograms will come into use in about seven years. Libraries of video cassettes should be developed to their fullest during the interim. You can't video enough good material from your own TV. I want to have my own choice of programs. There has to be the necessary software available.

BURROUGHS: I audio record everything I can.

BOWIE: The media is either our salvation or our death. I'd like to think it's our salvation. My particular thing is discovering what can be done with media and how it can be used. You can't draw people together like one big huge family, people don't want that. They want isolation or a tribal thing. A group of eighteen kids would much rather stick together and hate the next eighteen kids down the block. You are not going to get two or three blocks joining up and loving each other. There are just too many people.

BURROUGHS: Too many people. We're in an overpopulated

situation, but the less people you have does not include the fact that they are still heterogeneous. They are just not the same. All this talk about a world family is a lot of bunk. It worked with the Chinese because they are very similar.

BOWIE: And now one man in four in China has a bicycle and that is pretty heavy considering what they didn't have before. And that's the miracle as far as they're concerned. It's like all of us having a jet plane over here.

BURROUGHS: It's because they are the personification of one character that they can live together without any friction. We quite evidently are not.

BOWIE: It is why they don't need rock & roll. British rock & roll stars played in China, played a dirty great field and they were treated like a sideshow. Old women, young children, some teenagers, you name it, everybody came along, walked past them and looked at them on the stand. It didn't mean a thing. Certain countries don't need rock & roll because they were so drawn together as a family unit. China has its mother-father figure—I've never made my mind up which—it fluctuates between the two. For the West, Jagger is most certainly a mother figure and he's a mother hen to the whole thing. He's not a cockadoodledoo; he's much more like a brothel keeper or a madame.

BURROUGHS: Oh, very much so.

BOWIE: He's incredibly sexy and very virile. I also find him incredibly motherly and maternal clutched into his bosom of ethnic blues. He's a white boy from Dagenham trying his damnedest to be ethnic. You see, trying to tart the rock business up a bit is getting nearer to what the kids themselves are like, because what I find, if you want to talk in the terms of rock, a lot depends on sensationalism and the kids are a lot more sensational than the stars themselves. The rock business is a pale shadow of what the kids lives are usually like. The admiration comes from the other side. It's all a reversal, especially in recent years. Walk down Christopher Street and then you wonder exactly what went wrong. People are not like James Taylor; they may be molded on the outside, but inside their heads it is something completely different.

BURROUGHS: Politics of sound.

BOWIE: Yes. We have kind of got that now. It has very loosely shaped itself into the politics of sound. The fact that you can now subdivide rock into different categories was something that you couldn't do ten years ago. But now I can reel off at least ten sounds that represent a kind of person rather than a type of music. The critics don't like to say that, because critics like being critics, and most of them wish they were rock & roll stars. But when they classify they are talking about people, *not* music. It's a whole political thing.

BURROUGHS: Like infrasound, the sound below the level of hearing. Below 16 Hertz. Turned up full blast it can knock down walls for thirty miles. You can walk into the French patent office and buy the patent for 40p. The machine itself can be made very cheaply from things you could find in a junk yard.

BOWIE: Like black noise. I wonder if there is a sound that can put things back together. There was a band experimenting with stuff like that; they reckon they could make a whole audience shake.

BURROUGHS: They have riot-control noise based on these soundwaves now. But you could have music with infrasound, you wouldn't necessarily have to kill the audience.

BOWIE: Just maim them.

BURROUGHS: The weapon of the Wild Boys is a bowie knife, an eighteen-inch bowie knife, did you know that?

BOWIE: An eighteen-inch bowie knife . . . you don't do things by halves, do you. No, I didn't know that was their weapon. The name Bowie just appealed to me when I was younger. I was into a kind of heavy philosophy thing when I was sixteen years old, and I wanted a truism about cutting through the lies and all that.

BURROUGHS: Well, it cuts both ways, you know, double-edged on the end.

BOWIE: I didn't see it cutting both ways till now.

THE RAW AND UNCUT INTERVIEW

VOX POP
MARCH 18, 1987

VOX POP: So . . .

BOWIE: So.

VOX POP: Can we start by talking about Andy Warhol for a second?

BOWIE: Yeah, sure. Yeah.

VOX POP: What was his influence on your life and work?

BOWIE: I think it was more indirect than anything else. I mean, it was the fact that he was using a band, Velvet Underground, with his Exploding Plastic Inevitable—I can't remember, what was it called? Something like that wasn't it?

VOX POP: Um-hmm.

BOWIE: [*Laughs*] Now you're being the talking head.

VOX POP: The nodding head.

BOWIE: Um, and it was sort of by circuit that I got interested in the stuff that he was doing. Artistically, I thought it was interesting, sort of, um, it was a very bold step to take what he was doing—applying design values and graphics values to serious academic art. But it really was the inclusion of Velvet Underground as part of his whole entourage . . . team . . . I guess. But I didn't meet him until, I guess the early—late '60s, early '70s, I can't remember the year. I found him in, it was an incongruous kind of situation. The guy was in the Factory place, and it was a hive of activity, everybody was doing something, talking up this, talking up that. And the guy was just sort of very quiet. Sort of like a, a lethal kind of Svengali figure over this whole thing. Everything happened without his seeming to be taking any part in it. He was an extraordinary, hypnotic kind of guy.

VOX POP: Okay.

BOWIE: He was very, very funny, a very witty man, but it took long time before you got him talking.

VOX POP: So this was all before you wrote the song about him?

BOWIE: Yes it was, yeah, I—no, I wrote the Hunky Dory song before I met him. And then I played it to him at the Factory, and he said [*imitating Warhol*], "Oh yeah that's great." And that was his critique of the song. [*Laughs*] I don't know if he ever liked it or not.

VOX POP: All right. Let's go into the press conference today then . . .

BOWIE: Yeah.

VOX POP: . . . and why this approach? These live press conferences?*

BOWIE: Well, I tried it before in London, once upon a time, I did a press conference to announce the *Serious Moonlight* tour . . . and it was such a drag. I mean it felt so stiff and . . . and I just didn't like being up there doing it, and like I was just reading off dates. I just wanted to do something that was very comfortable this time, and I felt a lot more comfortable in a stage situation with the band with me and . . . um . . . and I'm playing music! I mean, that seems sort of—"Hey, here we are, this is what we're like, this is what it's about, it's about music, and this is what we sound like. We're a good club band!" [*Laughs*]

VOX POP: No it's great, it's like a tour preview. I think it got a lot of people excited. You're going to take this press conference thing around Europe, right?

BOWIE: Yeah.

---

* Bowie held a series of press conferences to preview his then-new album, *Never Let Me Down*.

VOX POP: . . . and I'm wondering which cities you're looking forward to the most.

BOWIE: For me, personally, it'll be Madrid and Rome, because I've never played either of them. I've been to Spain, and I've been to Italy, but only as a tourist. I've never played them before, so that'll be, I think, the most exciting ones for me to do.

VOX POP: The album seems like it is a lot more rocking and kind of noisy than the last two—

BOWIE: Yeah.

VOX POP: —and I'm wondering if you had playing live in mind while you recorded it?

BOWIE: Very much so. There were—two things were kind of ingredients for that whole thing: The *Serious Moonlight* period—that *Let's Dance* album—was, uh, Nile* did wonderful things for me on that album, he created an extraordinary sound. But with the inclusion of the horns and the, and the . . . *smoothness* of the whole deal, I started to become uncomfortable in carrying on with that direction, because I felt a little lost in that, and it was approaching an area that I didn't really feel I belonged in. And so coming to this album, I approached it from where—how I used to feel about bands

---

* Nile Rogers, the producer of the record.

when I started. I always go back—when you get lost you go back to point one. And so I approached the whole deal from what used to excite me about being in a band, and it just goes back to the guitar again. And so it became a guitar-oriented album. And as I was writing and feeling out the material I realized it was just a tremendous album to be touring, and so the whole thing meshed together, and I put the amount of energy that I needed into a *rock* album, to really make it happen on stage.

VOX POP: How about your musical role, because you didn't play instruments in the past two albums and now you're back to doing that.

BOWIE: Yeah, I've gone back to doing that because that was an integral part of what I used to do, and it produced the kind of sound that I really felt was *me*, because I was play-ing some of the stuff on it and I was kind of giving it some kind of foundation, on either the keyboards or a particular kind of rhythm guitar that I play—which is not like Carlos's [Alomar]—but it works! You know, I mean, it's not great, but it works! And so I wanted to kind of return to that. So I was happy to be—it was nice to be back in the band in that way, you know?

VOX POP: Was this one of those albums where you left a lot up to the band, or was it very much directed by you?

BOWIE: No, it's very, very structured, this one. I made demos of everything before we went in, and I played them to everybody and I said, "I want it to sound exactly like this but better." [*Laughs*] Because I played everything. I programmed drum machines and then played bass and guitar, keyboards and synthesizer parts. I did the whole deal on the demos and then I played the demos to Carlos, and Erdal Kızılçay, who's the drummer, and the bass player, and the synthesizer player, [*laughing*] and the trumpet player, and the string player on that album, and Peter [Frampton], and I said "This is where I'm going. That's the approach I want." And the demos are not dissimilar from this final album—except, of course that it's played much better. [*Laughs*]

VOX POP: How did Frampton get involved in this album?

BOWIE: He and I go back an awful long time, as I mentioned earlier. We met at school together and all that. He was younger than me, he was about [*clicks his tongue loudly*], let's see, he must have been about twelve, thirteen when I was fifteen. And he was only at the school a short time because his father was at the school, and he was my art master, and I think it was pretty tough on Pete, as it is for any kid if his father's the teacher at the school, you know? So he eventually left that school and went on to another one. But at the time, in the art block, that used to be like where all the musos hang out, you know, we used to bring our guitars to school. When we weren't painting we were playing guitar. And he used to come in over there and play over there, and he was just dynamite. I mean, already at thirteen he was a *great* guitarist. And then he went on and eventually went through the Herd and the Small Faces and all that.

And I kept running into him. We played with each other at various times. I was supporting him one time when he was with Humble Pie, and then he supported me at another time on another gig. And uh . . . all the way through I saw this dreadful stuff happening to him in the '70s—I mean, it was all getting lost that he was a great guitarist. He was suddenly a pop hero, and then he was a face. And the camera just moved up from the fingers right up here [*frames his face with his hands*] you know, and it was this all the time. And he hated that. And I know how he felt about that because sometimes my songwriting got lost along with, you know—but that was probably my fault because I was pushing everything else so hard, theatricality and all that.

And then, last year it became apparent that Peter was really back on the trail again with the Stevie Nicks tour, and really wanted to play. And I thought, gee, that's the guitarist I'd *really* like to work with on this next album, because he is great, and I'd give him a call. And I gave him a call and he'd said he'd love to do the album. And whilst we were doing the album the inevitable thing came up and he said, "Are you taking this stuff on the road?" And I said, "Yeah, do you think you want to come with it?" And he said "Yeah, that would be great!" And I said, "You don't mind just being in the back?" And he said, "No, I'd love to do it." And so, it really gives him a chance to showcase his talents as a guitarist, and then inevitably he'll go out on his own next year, and with a bit of luck people will know him for what he is— which is a great guitarist. And a very good songwriter and singer, as it happens. But it'll bring his guitar playing back into the forefront.

VOX POP: What is it about his playing? Is it melody—what?

BOWIE: It's a good combination of, um, because his musical background is very similar to mine, there's a sort of an English R&B awareness with all the R&B stuff that he used to play, so there's a certain contained roughness to his playing which I like very much— [*Phone rings*]

VOX POP: We're gonna have to do this over and if you could include Peter's name in the answer.

BOWIE: Oh, sure. Yeah, yeah, I understand . . . [*Waits for the crew, idly clicking his tongue loudly*] . . . Is a cigarette going to break up continuity?

VOX POP: No, no.

BOWIE: Dying for one! [*Laughing, assuming a gruff Cockney as he gets out his cigarettes and lights up*] When you start singing you really have to keep smoking you know, or it all goes! [*Holding out his cigarette pack to the crew*] Do you need that?

VOX POP: No, no.

BOWIE: Out of interest, you guys don't have a problem with the video do you? The "Day-In Day-Out"*?

---

* The video for the first single off the *Never Let Me Down* album.

VOX POP: No, the world premiere is tonight.

BOWIE: Great, thank you very much.

VOX POP: Let's pick up with Frampton again and what it is about his playing that you like so much

BOWIE: Peter's playing owes a lot to the rhythm and blues influences that we all had back in England in the '60s. But it's an English approach to the blues, you know? I mean it produced the Claptons, some of the very best blues guitarists in fact came out of England. And I always thought that Peter was one of them, and he just got lost along the way. Along with—you know, Beck was making a reputation, Clapton and all the others. And nothing really happened for Peter apart from [*imitating the sound*] the voicebox thing. And it's the kind of guitar playing that I've always really felt happiest with. [Mick] Ronson was the kind of guitarist I liked working with because it was about American music, but it was played with an English approach. And that's really what I like about Peter's playing. He's also incredibly open to ideas, and I dare say that I'll be working with him on all kinds of new approaches to what we can do with his guitar style on my material, anyway.

VOX POP: Okay great. Now let's get into the "Day-In Day-Out" video.

BOWIE: Yeah.

VOX POP: Now what was the idea behind it?

BOWIE: The subject matter generally, if I can preface that with the subject matter generally on the album, seems to be split between personal romance, personal feelings of love and, uh . . . some kind of statement or indictment of an uncaring society on this—particularly the response to what's happening in major cities, in terms of the homeless, of people who are just totally uncared for in terms of education or being fed properly or being housed properly. There's such a diversity of political stance now where the high power authorities seem to be far more concerned about the relations with Russia, or the Middle East, and the whole idea of what's happening at home on the streets with the indigenous population seems to be swept under the carpet. I'm not very—I'm not consciously, uh . . . *prolific* in terms of didactic statements. I mean, I would leave that very much to the Clash kind of band, or Dylan or the kind of, the way that Lennon would work with his songs. My things tend far more towards an impressionistic, almost surrealistic approach to statement.

But that's the body of the hour, I mean that's kind of the sense I was trying to get over on it. And "Day-In Day-Out" particularly dealt with the idea of somebody in a prejudiced position, in a position where there doesn't seem to be any kind of hope—it's impossible to make any money, it's impossible to get a good education . . . and the things that people unfortunately have to resort to try and get through, and in the end when the chips are down everything's awful. When you think you've got to the bottom of the pit it gets even worse, you know, and it's like there seems to be no way out from that situation. So that's kind of—does that make any sense? That's kind of my approach to that song. It really is about the effects of an uncaring society.

VOX POP: Now there's two different endings in the clip?

BOWIE: Not that I'm aware of. As far as I'm aware of, there's one ending.

VOX POP: 'Cause it's with the blocks, like in on one of them it says "fuck" or something, and the other one says "love"?

BOWIE: Oh yeah, yeah, yeah. We thought that was, you know, we thought we'd try—You know, as the battering machine comes through the window, on the first version that we shot, the kid's just putting his last block in the hole and he's like "Oh, *fuck*!" You know, like, "Great, after all this, this is really what we need." But we just knew that because of things being how they are on media, if we expected to get the thing played at all we'd put in the letter "L" instead, so it became "luck." Which is kind of almost better in a way. But I think we're probably sending both versions around and it's really up to the stations if they want, which version—some countries like Italy and France, of course, they don't care, they'll play the original. But America has, you know, it has its problems in that area, so what do you do? *Friday Night Video** particularly have problems in that area, because they're not used to seeing women in bras and panties . . .

VOX POP: What's that? Ah, no bras, huh.

---

* An NBC television show started in the early 1980s in an attempt to capitalize on the explosive popularity then of MTV.

BOWIE: No bras.

VOX POP: So, were you doing a clip with Mondino?*

BOWIE: Yes I did. There's a love song on the album called "Never Let Me Down," which is [*slipping into macho American accent*] it's the title track you know, it's like a real heavy romantic piece. I'm better off with that kind of stuff. [*Resumes normal voice*] And I thought it would be—he would be absolutely ideal. I'm not used to giving over my video authority to somebody so completely because I usually collaborate intensely with whoever I'm working with on the video. I storyboard myself, I usually conceive the thing myself, and then Julien Temple, or, in the past, David Mallet, have worked with me on how to get the best visual on my approach to the video. But with Mondino, he works in his own, he's in another world—the guy's so French, such a romantist, I can't get anywhere near where he's at in terms of direction, and so I just gave the whole thing over to him and I put myself really in his hands in terms of that video. But it's quite beautiful, quite lovely, and it's something I could never do. I could never make anything like that myself.

VOX POP: Because the song is kind of Lennon-esque, almost

---

* Jean-Baptiste Mondino is a French fashion photgrapher and video director.

like a John Lennon ballad, and I'm wondering what John Lennon told you about writing songs that stuck with you so much?

BOWIE: We talked about it, and, well the two things that I remember very strongly about it—well firstly, John was an extraordinary raconteur. I mean he could tell story after story. But he was quite adroit at keeping things short and simple and cutting right through bullshit and coming straight to the point with great one-liners. I mean he was a one-liner king. He had some wonderful one-liners. But the two major things that I remember he said about songwriting—when I first met him in the early '70s I said, "Well, what do you think about what I do?" I said, "Do you like all this glam rock stuff?" You know? And he said, "Yeah it's great. Well, it's just rock-n-roll with lipstick on, isn't it?" [*Laughing*] Which was so right—in one way. And then later on we were talking about songs and he said, you know, basically, what you need to do with a song is say what you mean, put a rhythm to it, and put a back beat to it. And that's it, and it really is as simple as that. And I understood that—I don't take that completely to heart because my way of working is not quite like that, but if I'm getting stuck, if I'm in a corner with a song or a piece of work and I've blanked out and I can't approach it in any way, I always go back to things that John said or things that Brian Eno said to me. I mean, he was also very helpful in terms of opening me up as a writer and changing my ideas about how I can write songs.

VOX POP: How so?

BOWIE: How so? With Brian particularly the whole idea of using a recording studio as an instrument. Of not necessarily thinking you have to be prepared totally before you go in. That accidents will happen, and sometimes planned accidents work out really well. If there's a bad note, you can layer that note several times with other instruments, and suddenly that bad note sounds like an extraordinary piece of arrangement. Those kind of things that are real, I guess—Brian is marvelous at the obvious; he'll say an obvious thing, but you would never have thought of it before.

VOX POP: Okay, could we talk about your movies for a little bit? I mean you've played so many different roles in your films, but I'm wondering what to you is the thread running through them all?

BOWIE: Ninety percent of the time I've only ever taken a role on, firstly, if it's a reasonably good role, but primarily because of the director involved, because I wanted to see how he worked, and what his chemistry was with the relationships with his crew, how he put things together. And that applies to just about every director that I've worked with really. That's a thread. Character threads I don't know, I like characters that are just slightly off the wall, I think.

VOX POP: Well which one is the most like you and which one is the least like you?

BOWIE: The one that's most like me . . . ? [*Laughing*] I suppose the nerd in *Blue Jean*.* I think there's a nerd busting out of me. There's a . . . I kind of felt very at one with the sneaky little gangster guy in *Into the Night*, the cameo thing that I did for John Landis—I've got great empathy with that character. [*Laughs*] The least like me I guess, I hope anyway, is *The Hunger*. I felt very uncomfortable with that role, although I loved being involved in a Tony Scott movie. I thought Tony was tremendous, absolutely tremendous. And his *second* film being *Top Gun*, I thought why did you give me your *first* film, Tony? But these things happen. I think the same thing will happen with Julien by the way on the *Absolute Beginners* thing, which I personally love. I think it's a great little movie. It's a very new approach to making movies. But the same thing will happen with Julien is that—frankly, Tony, nobody would touch him after *The Hunger*. For years! And then suddenly he gets *Top Gun*, and now he's just done *Beverly Hills Cop II*, and the guy's like the biggest thing since sliced bread in America. And the same thing will happen with Julien, I know it. He'll make his next film, maybe not the next one, *maybe* the next one, and suddenly Julien will be on the map again, you know? It's such a fickle thing with film. It really is.

VOX POP: What did you learn from Nicolas Roeg?

BOWIE: Nic Roeg, I think . . . I still think he's the only director that I've worked with that the sum of the parts that

---

* A twenty-minute short film promoting Bowie's song of the same title, directed by Julien Temple.

he puts in, there is something *greater* that he evolves out of that. His work has a certain alchemy, a certain chemistry in it, that I've never really seen with any of the other directors that I've worked with. There's some kind of magic ingredient that he puts in. His combinations of quick shots and quick flashes that, when you build up his imagery, it focuses into another world. He creates this spatial area between reality and the spiritual life, and he puts you somewhere in the middle. The nearest I've really seen to it, in terms of magic, is David Lynch, who I admire very much indeed. And Alex Cox I like a lot. I think Alex Cox is just tremendous.

VOX POP: Okay, the way you look now—

BOWIE: Yeah?

VOX POP: The leather jacket and everything—it's really nice. Why are you looking like that these days?

BOWIE: I think you've got to be pretty emphatic and up-front and forward about what you're trying to do and what you're trying to say in rock and roll, and it's a people's culture, so I don't think it's too wise to be too clever. I'm going to do a rock and roll tour this year. The only statement that I can make visually with clothes that is not fashion is this. This is totally non-fashion—it's timeless, and I feel very comfortable in it, doing what I'm doing, writing the music that I'm writing. And of course I've always worn this jacket.

VOX POP: Okay, now the Beatles. How much did the Beatles affect the way you looked and dressed back in the early to mid-sixties?

BOWIE: Not at all. I wasn't a Beatles clothes fan at all. No, I never—I was more into the Who and all of that. I mean, I was very much a mod in the sixties, you know? It was all hair and the right Fred Perry T-shirts and the length of the trouser had to be just so and all that. I mean it was all very sort of French. The whole mod look in England came out of French fashion and at that time was really good for guys: French fashion and Italian fashion. But it became like the mod look. So I was much more into that than I was into sort of Beatle jackets and stuff.

DAVID BOWIE: STARDUST MEMORIES

REFLECTIONS ON A LIFE OF WIT AND STYLE

INTERVIEW BY KURT LODER
ROLLING STONE
APRIL 23, 1987

For fifteen years, David Bowie has been the ringmaster of rock style, whipping up new fashions and attitudes with every flick of his public image. A prodigy of self-invention, he has been at various intervals Art Man, Dance Man, and Pioneer Androgyne. Today he's just plain David, but the contemporary urban clubscape is still littered with Bowie replicants bearing painted witness to the lingering influence of his past personas: whole tribes of bleached and preening Ziggys, plucked and pallid Aladdins, sleek, cadaverous Euro-lizards. But the man behind those masks has long since moved on.

As he sat down for an interview in a suite at a Westwood hotel one recent afternoon, Bowie was wearing simple black jeans, a snug tank-top T-shirt, and steel-toed Gaultier brogues, it was February, one month after his fortieth birthday, and Bowie was in Los Angeles to shoot videos for his seventeenth studio album, *Never Let Me Down*. Clear-eyed and lightly tanned beneath a generous thatch of blond-plus hair, he looked astonishingly fit and professed his eagerness to wade back into the rock-biz fray. He'll kick off a world tour in June, performing songs drawn from the breadth of his twenty-year recording career, backed by a band featuring his old pal Peter Frampton—the son of Bowie's high school art teacher—on lead. It will, he said, be something special.

The subject was rock style, of which Bowie is pretty much the reigning embodiment. Born on January 8, 1947, and raised in districts of Brixton and Bromley, he is old enough to have witnessed firsthand the arrival of rock & roll. As a kid, he marveled at the brawling, zoot-suited antics of the Teddy boys, England's first rock-oriented youth cult. In the Sixties, he took up the saxophone, joined a school band (the Konrads), and felt himself drawn toward the clothes-obsessed mods, who shared his musical taste for American R&B. He idolized such British beat legends as the $ély Who and the Yardbirds (whose lead singer, Keith Relf, inspired him to grow his hair down to his shoulders). As Davy Jones, he hacked around with a succession of groups— the King Bees, the Manish Boys, the Lower Third—to little avail. Advised in 1966 that another Davy Jones had hit it big as a member of the Monkees, he adopted the stage name Bowie and went solo. He recorded his first album in 1967 and scored his first hit single—the trippy "Space Oddity"— two years later.

Bowie's breakthrough came in 1972, with the release of *The Rise and Fall of Ziggy Stardust and the Spiders from Mars*, an album of hard, snarling guitar rock pumped out by what may have been the best band he has ever had [lead guitarist Mick Ronson, bassist Trevor Bolder, and drummer Woody Woodmansey, three musicians from the north of England, with American keyboardist Mike Garson added to the lineup a bit later]. The main attraction, though, was Bowie's pan-caked, mock-mincing Ziggy persona—a character that came to define the glitter-rock era of the early Seventies. [Bowie occasionally appeared in public wearing dresses and at one point even told a reporter that he was gay—a statement he disavowed in a 1983 interview with *Rolling Stone*.]

Ziggy grew ever more alien over the course of such subsequent LPs as *Aladdin Sane* and *Pin-Ups* (a terrific col-lection of oldie remakes). By the time of 1974's *Diamond Dogs*—the cover of which depicted David with the body of a dog—Bowie was feeling burned out: wasted by heavy cocaine use and increasingly isolated by the MainMan orga-nization, a production office set up by his drug-disdaining manager, Tony DeFries, but staffed by high-living trendies recruited from Andy Warhol's Factory axis, among them ex-groupie Cherry Vanilla and future biographer Tony Zanetta. Weary and confused, he hired a new personal assistant—Corinne "Coco" Schwab, the multilingual daughter of a noted French photographer, who had been raised in India, Haiti, and Mexico and thus shared Bowie's own general sense of statelessness. He then split from MainMan and in 1975, with disco on the rise, suddenly slicked back his hair, suited up, and released the ultradanceable *Young Americans*, an album of what Bowie called "plastic soul." The following year came *Station to Station* and yet another new character: the skeletal and decadent Thin White Duke. Bowie also starred in Nicolas Roeg's movie *The Man Who Fell to Earth* [inaugurating an erratic film career that includes 1978's *Just a Gigolo*, a resounding bomb; 1983's *The Hunger*, a campy vampire flick directed by Tony Scott, and *Merry Christmas,*

Mr. Lawrence, a memorable prisoner-of-war movie directed by the esteemed Japanese filmmaker Nagisa Oshima; and 1986's *Labyrinth*, a goblin fantasy directed by Jim Henson, and *Absolute Beginners*, a musical fiasco by video wiz Julien Temple]. Bowie moved to Berlin, began listening to such German synthesizer groups as Kraftwerk, and in 1977 released the first of a trio of largely brilliant art-rock collaborations with former Roxy Music synth avatar Brian Eno [*Low*, *"Heroes,"* and *Lodger*].

By 1980, a new cult of fashion-crazed kids—the New Romantics—had sprouted up in London. Bowie walked among them [they were his stylistic children, in many ways] and came back with *Scary Monsters (and Super Creeps)*, an album that, unfortunately, yielded no major hits. Was he running out of steam? Bowie answered that question with an emphatic no in 1983, when he dropped all his guises and went dance pop with *Let's Dance*, the biggest-selling album of his career.

Bowie was married for nearly ten years to Angela Barnet, an Anglo-American woman with whom he had a son, Zowie (now called Joe). Their union, hardly strengthened by David's dalliance with such girlfriends as black singer Ava Cherry, dissolved in divorce in 1980. Today, David lives with Coco and Joe—who'll be sixteen in May—in a house in Switzerland, not far from the jet-set resort of Gstaad, where Bowie frequently skis. He also works out and roller-skates in his spare time—of which there's never much: he remains a workaholic. Despite his now-moneyed seclusion, he remains an artist with one ear—and one shrewd fashion eye—ever cocked toward the street, ever alert for the latest innovations. At last glance, however, no likely usurpers had appeared to challenge Bowie's position as the king of rock style.

• • •

LODER: First of all, a belated happy birthday.

BOWIE: Thank you!

LODER: Has turning forty made you reflective?

BOWIE: No, not at all. Now I feel I can do and say what I want. [*Laughs*]

LODER: Were you aware of style as a kid?

BOWIE: Yes, I liked how things went together, and it interested me how it all worked. But I think I was always drawn to the crass [*chuckles*], so that saved my ass, really: I was never very hot on sophisticated taste when it got too sophisticated. I didn't mind a sense of elegance and style, but I liked it when things were a bit off—a bit sort of fish-and-chips shop

LODER: Were you aware of the Teds when they appeared?

BOWIE: Yeah. There was a bloke who lived down the road from us who was a Ted—Eric, I think his name was. He had brilliant, curly ginger hair and razor blades in his collar—for purposes of not being molested, I guess, by other Teds. That

I found very impressive. But he was slightly potty—he would just stand on the corner for hours, swinging a chain manically.

LODER: Were you ever inclined toward Teddishness yourself?

BOWIE: Yeah, a lot of kids my age got into those things. But I didn't really like the Teddy clothes too much. I liked Italian stuff. I was *really* early into Italian stuff. I liked the box jackets and the mohair. You could get *some* of that locally in Bromley, but not very good. You'd have to go right up to Shepherd's Bush or the East End. And once I'd left school, you could save a little money and go find a tailor who would make it up really well. There were some good tailors. The one I used to go to was the same one that Marc Bolan used to go to, a fairly well known one in Shepherd's Bush. I remember I saved up and got one suit made there, but that was really all. The rest of my money I put into equipment and saxophones and things.

LODER: There's a picture of you with the Kon-rads where you have this sort of upswept crew cut . . .

BOWIE: Oh, yes, yes. I loved the hair-style stuff, yeah.

LODER: And the band is wearing, like, little candy-striped ties . . .

BOWIE: We wore gold corduroy jackets, I remember, and brown mohair trousers and green, brown, and white ties, I think, and white shirts. *Strange* coloration.

LODER: Was there a particular rock performer who had really turned you on as a kid? Someone you saw and said, "That's what I want to do"?

BOWIE: Little Richard. I saw him at Brixton Odeon. It must have been 1963, 'cause the Stones opened for him. I'll tell you who else was on that bill, as well. Oh, it was wonderful, listen: The Stones opened, then there was Bo Diddley and, if I remember rightly, Duane Eddy, and it closed with Sam Cooke. That was the first half. Then the second half . . . Who else was on that thing? Somebody else unbelievable was on, and *then* Little Richard. And Little Richard was *just unreal.* Unreal. Man, we'd never seen *any-thing* like that. It was still mohair suits then—I mean, just *great* suits—baggy trousers and all that. And he was workin' with a British band called Sounds Incorporated—our only horn band, the only band that knew anything about saxo-phones. There was one other, Peter Jay and the Jaywalkers, but they weren't as good. Sounds Incorporated were the one. And I think it was probably Red Price on tenor sax, guy with dark glasses. I used to love all those sax players, 'cause that's what I wanted to do. And he led Lord Rock-ingham's XI, too. [*Laughs*] Remember them? "Hoots, mon, there's a moose loose about this hoose!" You don't remem-ber that?

Anyway, that show was unreal. And the Stones were so funny. They had, like, four fans at that time, who *rushed* down the aisles to the front. These four chicks in the front there—it was *so* funny. Keith was dynamite, 'cause he did that aeroplane stuff in those days, whizzing round and round—he really made an entrance. And Brian was kind of dominant in the band then; he really was. It's amazing the progress that Mick's made, thinking back, because as stage personalities, Mick and Brian were equal. And some bloke—I'll never forget this—some bloke in the audience looked at Jagger and said, "Get your hair cut!" And Mick said, "What—and look like *you*?" It was *so funny*! I went with the Kon-rads, and we just collapsed in our seats.

LODER: What kind of stuff did the Kon-rads play?

BOWIE: Lotta covers. And then . . . the band broke up because of me, actually. Yes, folks, I broke the Kon-rads up—now it can be told!

LODER: Why did you do that?

BOWIE: I wanted to do rhythm & blues songs, and nobody was interested. I remember the first one I really tried to get them to do—and I wish we'd done it, 'cause it would've done rather well—was "House of the Rising Sun," off an old blues album that got released in England.

LODER: In 1963? You were ahead of your time.

BOWIE: Eh! It was so great, and I wanted to put a beat to it. But I rather got beaten to that.

LODER: What about the Manish Boys, that seven-piece group you were in till early 1965?

BOWIE: That was just survival. I didn't really like that band at all. It was rhythm & blues, but it wasn't very good.

Nobody ever earned any money. The band was so huge; it was dreadful. And I had to live in Maidstone. That's where the Manish Boys were from, and so I had to go and live there, because we were gonna rehearse and work outta there. I don't know if you know Maidstone. Maidstone Prison is one of the biggest in England. It's all criminals round there—one prison and a few suburban houses. It's the only time in my life I've ever been beaten up.

LODER: By whom?

BOWIE: By some ex-prisoner, I suppose. I don't know. It was just this big herbert walkin' down the street just knocked me on the pavement, and when I fell down, proceeded to kick the *shit* outta me. For no reason that I could fathom to this day. I haven't got many good memories of Maidstone.

That wasn't a long-lived band, though, the Manish Boys. But I affected a Keith Relf haircut, I believe, at the time. I was quite keen on Keith. I thought he was pretty cool—my favorite R&Ber. I liked the Who's sound but Keith Relf's look. I thought, "If I can get that down, wow—watch out world." [*Laughs*]

LODER: Was the Lower Third, your next band, a happier affair?

BOWIE: The Lower Third was very Who inspired.

LODER: Did you do Who covers?

BOWIE: No, we wrote our own stuff. I was fully into writing by then. I was absolutely convinced that I could write anything as good as anybody else, have a go at it.

LODER: And proved yourself right, eventually.

BOWIE: Yeah, that's right—see, Pete! [*Laughs*] I took my first single to Pete Townshend. It was at a Who concert in 1969—must have been around there—and I took it and I got backstage and I gave it to him. I said, "Play that and let me know what you think of it one day." And it was many years later he said, "By the way, son, I remember you bringing me that single. I meant to let you know—I did like it." Lyin' bastard! [*Laughs*]

LODER: Were you much of a mod?

BOWIE: Yeah. Oh, absolutely.

LODER: I mean, were you deeply into it?

BOWIE: Not deeply into the lifestyle. Superficially. Because I didn't like riding scooters. And I was never too much of a club guy—never really went clubbing very much.

LODER: Really?

BOWIE: No. Like once a week or something. Which actually, in that time, was not very much. I mean, those kids used to go every night and hang out till seven in the morning. I liked going to art museums and bits of theater, things like that. I wasn't really that concerned with *that* many clubs.

LODER: But you picked up on the mod clothes?

BOWIE: Yeah.

LODER: Where would you buy them?

BOWIE: Let me see. At that time, I suppose sport shops and things. Like now. See, that's come back full cycle. A lot of mods used to wear sports clothes—Fred Perry shirts and things like that. Um . . . Carnaby Street was *briefly* popular, for like a three-month period or something; then it fast became . . .

LODER: What it is today—a sort of tourist slum?

BOWIE: Yeah, exactly. And then of course the Kings Road also had its time, you know? But they were all sort of very fast. I didn't really have a hangout for clothes. I didn't wear much that was fashionable, actually. I mean, I was quite happy with things like Fred Perrys and a pair of slacks. Not very loud clothes.

LODER: Did flower power pretty much sweep everything else away, fashionwise?

BOWIE: Yeah, I think everybody did become psychedelic, at least. I don't really remember the people that I knew being that affected by the love-and-peace things about it. They were *definitely* affected by the mushroom aspects, and the colors and all that—the clothes and the psychedelic music. But love and peace, I felt, was very much the American part of it all. It certainly made its impression in the hit parade, but it was very commercial oriented—you know: "If you're going to San Francisco," that kind of stuff. And we had bands like the Flowerpot Men. There was a lot of that about. But the best aspects of it were some of the early things that Jeff Beck did, you know? Now, that's what I liked about it—that was really good stuff.

LODER: Your Ziggy Stardust persona was a daring departure for rock. What were those early shows like?

BOWIE: What was quite hard was dragging the rest of the band into wanting to do it.

LODER: They were pretty much rock & roll, pub kind of guys?

BOWIE: Yeah, we always had that problem. That was the major problem, that we really didn't think alike at all. It was like, "Jesus, come on, you lot—let's not just be another rock band, for Christ's sakes." [*Laughs*] But they were a *great* little rock band, you know? And they caught on to it as soon as they found that they could pull more girls. Then it was, "Hey, they *like* these boots." I thought, "Yeah, there you go." That's what it needed. God—get a bit of sex into it and they were *away*, boy. Their hair suddenly got . . . oh, it was every color under the sun. All these guys that wouldn't get out of denims until two weeks ago. [*Laughs*]

LODER: Where did the clothes for the Ziggy period come from? Did you design them yourself?

BOWIE: No, that was a designer whose clothes I saw, a guy named Kansai Yamamoto. Now, of course, he's an international designer, but he was very experimental at that time—his stuff was way off the board. So the very first things were influenced by him, and then I got to know him, and he made all the stuff you really know—the suits, the pull-apart stuff, all those things. He said, "Oh, this band are weird—*tee-hee-hee*—they wear my clothes."

LODER: How did audiences respond to the early Ziggy shows, before the Ziggy Stardust album actually came out?

BOWIE: There was quite a bit of antagonism. Nothing like, say, the Pistols got when they started. But the first couple of months were not easy. The people did find it very hard, until we had a musical breakthrough. The actual look and everything, I mean, it was "Aw, a bunch of poofters," you know? Which was kind of fun. I mean, we played it up—well, I did, anyway—played that up a lot. Because it was the most rebellious thing that was happening at the time.

LODER: Is it true that when Ziggy and the Spiders played Santa Monica on the first tour, the band went off to a Scientology meeting and got converted?

BOWIE: Well, two of the band *are* Scientologists now. Mike Garson always *was* a Scientologist. I mean, Mike was a real hard nut to deal with, a very strange cat. I mean, he spent *all* his time tryin' to convert everybody—it was kind of difficult to work with him, you know? And he converted Woody Woodmansey, the drummer. Mike got him. He tried it on me for a bit, until we had a bit of a fight about it. He said, "Oh, well, you'd never understand, you're a druggie." I said, "Yeah, that's it—drugs are keepin' me away from Scientology." He was so po-faced. Very serious guy.

LODER: You had conceived Ziggy as the ultimate plastic rock star; ironically, the music that "he" made was really great.

BOWIE: I know, I know. It sounds all right now, yeah. I find it ironic when I look at a band, say, like Sigue Sigue Sputnik, where it's *so outré*, so *absolutely* in the Ziggy court, you know? All this time later, it still raises its brightly colored head.

LODER: Like psychedelia: it never goes away.

BOWIE: Yeah. That whole period, I guess. They keep recycling *all* of us—Roxy, me, Gary Glitter, Marc Bolan. I guess those four were the big ones from England, the champions of the early Seventies and all that. But it really seems to have permeated every area of rock now—something that one of us did is somewhere in all modern music. Which is *great*. I think that's fabulous.

LODER: Like Prince, maybe?

BOWIE: Prince, yeah, sure. I mean, he's probably *the* most, eclectic artist I've seen since *me*. [*Laughs*] I think he's a *great* stealer.

LODER: Was Aladdin Sane meant to be a conscious modulation on the Ziggy character or something completely different?

BOWIE: It was meant to be . . . a crossover: getting out of Ziggy and not really knowing where I was going. It was a little ephemeral, 'cause it was certainly up in the air.

LODER: Did you design the Aladdin Sane makeup yourself?

BOWIE: I came up with the flash thing on the face.

LODER: What was that meant to be?

BOWIE: Lightning bolt. An electric kind of thing. Instead of, like, the flame of a lamp, I thought he would probably be cracked by lightning. Sort of an obvious-type thing, as he was sort of an electric boy. But the teardrop was Brian Duffy's, an English artist-photographer. He put that on afterward, just popped it in there. I thought it was rather sweet.

LODER: And how did Aladdin Sane then mutate into the *Diamond Dogs* period?

BOWIE: Christ knows! I know the impetus for *Diamond Dogs* was both *Metropolis* and *1984*—those were the two things that went into it. In fact, *Diamond Dogs* was gonna be a rewrite of *1984*—I wanted to try to get the musical rights for it and turn it into a stage musical for touring. But my office, MainMan, didn't bother to do anything about it, and then I found out that if I dared touch it, Mrs. George Orwell would sue or something. So I suddenly had to change about in midstream, in the middle of recording, you know? But, I mean . . . well, it wasn't a real office in those days. Nobody did anything.

LODER: In 1973, midway between *Aladdin Sane* and *Diamond Dogs*, you released *Pin-Ups*, a collection of cover versions of your favorite oldies. A lot of people still think it's one of your best records. Might you ever do another one like it?

BOWIE: Yeah, I'm dying to do that. But I'd want to do it properly, not just as a filler between albums, you know? I really want to do it. 'Cause I've always made lists of things that I want to cover one day, and those lists go on and on and on. So it would be easy to just drop one in. I think the best time to do it would be at the end of a tour, when you're really up and you've still got the energy to do some high-energy performances. I'm so tempted—*this* is the time.

LODER: What songs would you like to cover?

BOWIE: I'm not gonna tell ya! [*Laughs*] 'Cause I've got some beauts that nobody'd ever *dream* of doing.

LODER: *Young Americans*, the studio album that followed *Diamond Dogs* in 1975, marked a brand-new artistic direction for you—deep into black American dance rhythms. What do you make of the current state of black pop?

BOWIE: There's nobody that's knockin' me out. I'm not in there with Lionel anymore. I liked Cameo's "Word Up" and then I heard the album and I just went to sleep. Rap is really the only cutting edge at the moment—Run-D.M.C. are my favorites. But I have a tough time with a lot of black music now—it's all a bit dancey, and there's no real underbelly there, you know? I think Prince is probably the best of the current crop.

LODER: Did you see his second movie, *Under the Cherry Moon*?

BOWIE: Yeahhh . . . I saw it. I'm not gonna say a thing. I mean, I've had so many of those myself, I wouldn't even *dream*. It'd be the pot callin' the kettle black, you know? *Whoops!* [*Laughs*]

LODER: In 1976, you moved to Berlin, and the following year, you began a new avant-garde period with the release of the *Low* and *"Heroes"* albums. What's your impression of the state of the musical avant-garde today?

BOWIE: Well, in America, it seems to have died.

LODER: It does seem very career oriented here.

BOWIE: That's an interesting thing. There's Philip Glass, who's now at the zenith of his professional bit, and Laurie

Anderson, who does TV and stage shows. In Germany, that period is over. I think it was starting to fold up on itself just around the time I left Berlin. The stuff that's coming out of Düsseldorf now is really boring.

LODER: What about Kraftwerk? You named one song on *"Heroes"* after that group's Florian Schneider. What do you think of its latest music?

BOWIE: It's its usual pristine self. And it's good, in its genre. But they're like craftsmen—they've decided they're gonna make this particular wooden chair that they designed, and each one will be very beautifully made, but it will be the same chair. It's like a cottage-industry thing. They're craftsmen.

LODER: Despite all the touring you did—and the critical acclaim you amassed—through that early part of your career, you wound up in considerable debt. How come?

BOWIE: It was all the MainMan tribe. Most of them wanted to be stars; so a lot of them were usin' the money that was comin' in—if it wasn't for drugs, it was to put their own stage productions together and things like that. I mean, there were more drugs goin' around—unbelievable. I thought I was bad, but it was just incredible how many drugs there were. And that's what happened to all the money.

LODER: You finally got the business side of your career together in 1983, when you signed a very lucrative contract with a new label and released your biggest LP, *Let's Dance.* How do you look at the music business today—as a game you've sort of mastered?

BOWIE: I had a few problems with it a couple of years ago, at the time of *Let's Dance* and just after. I suddenly had this huge audience that I'd never had before. I didn't quite know what I was supposed to do. So I just cut out last year—stayed in Europe, up in the mountains most of the time, writing and working, just doing the things that I really like. And that put me back on course. That's why I guess this new album sounds so much more . . . as though the continuity hasn't been broken from *Scary Monsters*. It's almost as though *Let's Dance* and *Tonight* were in the way there. And I'm going to do a stage thing this year, which I'm incredibly excited about, 'cause I'm gonna take a chance again.

LODER: Can you say what it might be?

BOWIE: *No!* [*Laughs*] Too many other acts are goin' out. I'll just be doing what I always did, which is keeping things interesting.

LODER: What do you actually do at home in Switzerland? It's a pretty quiet place, isn't it?

BOWIE: I work. All me time. If I'm not working, I ski. That's my only other preoccupation. I paint if I have the time or if I feel in the mood. And I read extensively.

LODER: What have you read recently?

BOWIE: I've just finished reading Joe Orton's plays. I also read Harold Pinter's *The Dumb Waiter*, which is a fabulous short play.

LODER: Have you ever met Pinter?

BOWIE: Lord, no. I'd love to meet him. Well, I *think* I'd like to meet him. Actually, I *hate* meeting famous people. It's always a letdown. They're a lot shorter than they look on television. [*Laughs*] Charlie Sexton's the only bloke I've met recently who's taller than I thought he was. No, hold on—there's a Duran who's like that as well: John Taylor. He's quite tall, yeah.

LODER: What do you make of the Durans? Are you buddies with them?

BOWIE: I had a hard time with them when I first met them a few years ago. I thought they were really sort of a bit arrogant. But I guess we all go through that. They've really got okay over the last year or two. Simon seems to have changed an *awful* lot since he seriously got back into sailing again. And since he changed his hair color. [*Laughs*]

LODER: Have you read these two recent books about you, *Bowie*, by Jerry Hopkins, and *Stardust*, by journalist Henry Edwards and your old MainMan employee Tony Zanetta?

BOWIE: The two books on me? Do you know that at last count there are thirty-seven? Thirty-seven, at the moment. I stopped reading those things after about the fourth or fifth one. Because once one saw the cast of characters, it became obvious that they were making a career out of it. The inevitable names would just keep coming up: the ex-wife, Ava Cherry, Cherry Vanilla, Tony Zanetta. Basically, all the people who had such a good time in the early Seventies and now are broke.

LODER: Have you ever been approached about doing your own book?

BOWIE: A *million* times. For *amazing* amounts of money.

LODER: Ever been tempted to do it?

BOWIE: Not in the least.

LODER: You started a feature-film career in 1976 with *The Man Who Fell to Earth*, and there've been five more movies since then. Are there any new films in the works that you can talk about?

BOWIE: Not really. Mick and I are always talkin' about doing one. I guess that probably will come off, but only if we can arrive at a story that we believe in doing, and not just being put together for an on-the-road movie or something like that.

LODER: You've been looking at scripts?

BOWIE: We're more concerned in writing something. That's what we're endeavoring to do. I think we've got to play it very carefully. It's got to be a story of some considerable substance, and inevitably it should have a lot of music in it. But I don't think it should have performance. Otherwise, it falls into that abyss of, you know, the celebrity rock & roll movie.

It's a difficult one, but I think we're cracking it. We are workin' on something, I've got to admit. We're working in conjunction with a writer that we respect a lot, so we'll see how it goes.

LODER: Is it difficult for someone like you—who deals in masks and personas onstage—to do film acting, to reveal himself to the camera?

BOWIE: No, it's not difficult for me. I don't know enough about it, so it's quite pleasant for me still. I don't have the burden of thinking, "I've got to better my last performance," you know? [*Laughs*] So I just enjoy it.

LODER: Were you happy with the way *Absolute Beginners* came out?

BOWIE: I *liked* that movie. I see it as another *Rocky Horror Picture Show*. I was in Tower Video the other day getting a couple of things, and they said that that film is one of *the* most rented movies. And kids come back sayin' they've learned the entire script of it. If that starts, and it starts goin' out into those late-night theaters, I can see it becoming one of those kinds of movies.

LODER: Well, it's not like any other movie.

BOWIE: [*Laughs*] No, it's not like any other movie. And Julien Temple, like Tony Scott . . . I mean, I had the pleasure of workin' with Tony on *The Hunger*—fortunately, we're still friends—and after *The Hunger*, he had *such* a tough time. People wouldn't even look at him. I mean, nobody ever suspected—least of all him, I think—that he would become the biggest director in America. One *Top Gun* [*snaps fingers*]— suddenly he's got *Beverly Hills Cop II*, and he's *it!* I *knew* he had incredible talent as a director. And I feel the same way about Julien—Julien *will* break through.

LODER: I always thought *The Hunger* would become a cult movie.

BOWIE: That rents pretty good, too. It's in that book, *Cult Movies*. Along with *Absolute Beginners*. Listen: *Absolute Beginners*, *The Hunger*, *The Man Who Fell to Earth*—they're *in* there, boy. [*Laughs*] Of *course* I looked!

LODER: Which of your films are your favorites?

BOWIE: *The Man Who Fell to Earth* I still think is a fascinating movie. And *Merry Christmas, Mr. Lawrence*, I guess. Those are the two I like the best. Although I do feel quite sympathetically towards *The Hunger* now. Yeah, there's some quite interesting stuff in that. I tell you, the first twenty minutes rattle along like hell—it really is a great opening. It loses its way about there, but it's still an interesting movie.

LODER: Everything lives on on video now. I think that's great.

BOWIE: Yeah. Well, for *some* it's great. [*Laughs*] They can lose *Just a Gigolo*, as far as I'm concerned. [*Laughs*]

LODER: That's probably in *Cult Movies*, isn't it?

BOWIE: I didn't even want to gaze at the J section. [*Laughs*]

LODER: Not a pleasant memory?

BOWIE: Well, it was, actually. I had more fun on that than any of them. Because we all looked at each other after a couple of weeks and said, "This is a piece of shit, isn't it?" "Yes." "Okay, let's just have a good time." So we had a great time in Berlin for the five or six weeks. But we *knew*.

LODER: Did you ever meet Rainer Werner Fassbinder during your time in Germany?

BOWIE: I never met him. I saw him once, in a bar.

LODER: Drunk?

BOWIE: No, he was all right. He was standing up. With a bunch of *really* heavy-looking guys. The kind of guys that the Hell's Angels would stay away from. I mean, he hung with a heavy crowd there—a heavy dude! But he was a fascinating guy. Extraordinary use of film, and the symbolic messages in it. Just incredible. I must say, I do have a penchant for the German filmmakers. Herzog is just fabulous as well.

LODER: Tina Sinatra recently said that you and Robert De Niro are the two people she has in mind to play her father, Frank Sinatra, in a film biography she's doing.

BOWIE: Which part of him would I play?

LODER: The English part, I suppose. She said that Frank "respects" you as an artist.

BOWIE: That's very decent. What an extraordinary thing.

LODER: Have you ever been offered the lead in any other biographical films?

BOWIE: Oh, funny things—like Byron, stuff like that. I don't know, I think Mick would do a better Byron. I'd probably be a better Shelley. [*Laughs*] But I don't think I'd like to do those kinds of things. I'd much prefer to do originally created stories for the screen—things that I could treat more seriously than some of the stuff I'm offered.

LODER: Do you think there are any movies that have really captured rock & roll on film?

BOWIE: I think probably *Sid & Nancy*, in a strangely macabre way. Those are the aspects that seem to grab people's attention, and it was a great film in those aspects. I thought the characterizations of some of the people around Sid were awful. I thought Iggy was ridiculous. I mean, did you see that as Iggy? It was incredible. The guy was like Neil Diamond or

something, in this big apartment with all these girls round
him. I've never seen Iggy like that in *my* life, and I'm sure the
Pistols never saw him like that either. And Johnny Rotten was
terrible. But Gary Oldman was good as Sid. I only met Sid
twice, I think.

LODER: How did he strike you as a person?

BOWIE: Just a mindless twerp. I didn't find anything at all
romantic about him, or even interesting. I think he was just
completely under the charisma of Rotten. Whatever Johnny
said, Sid would jump to it.

LODER: Did you ever see the Pistols live?

BOWIE: No. I just saw them because of my involvement with
Iggy, on his 1977 tour, when I was playing piano. And Johnny
and Sid—they all individually turned up to different shows,
you know? 'Cause, I mean, they just worshiped the ground
that Iggy . . . spat on. [*Chuckles*]

LODER: Ah, the old nihilism. You used to be very apocalypti-
cally minded, it seemed, back in the *Diamond Dogs* days. Do
you still feel that way—that the end is near?

BOWIE: No, I don't feel that at all. I *can't* feel that. I always
have to look for some kind of light at the end of the tun-
nel. Having a son does that. You change a lot. I think when
you're young, you feel it's kind of exciting to have that kind

of negative feeling about things. But that changes as you get older. That's the one thing that *does* change. The *energy* doesn't change; it just gets channeled in a different direction.

LODER: Do you think rock & roll has changed?

BOWIE: Rock & roll is for *us*—it's not for kids. *We* wrote it, *we* play it, *we* listen to it. *We* listen to rock. Kids listen to something else—they have a new need for music, in a different way.

LODER: Do you think rock is dead?

BOWIE: Purely on release of high spirits, it's still just as important as it was. But *socially*, it's changing its calendar; it's changing its vocabulary continually. Which is what makes it the most exciting art form, really. Because it *is* social currency; it actually has a place in society. It's a living art, and it is undergoing constant reevaluation and change. Which makes it far more interesting than, say, painting, or any of the plastic arts, which are so much for the few. And there's quite as much money attached to painting these days as there ever was in rock . . .

I think there's a refocusing in rock now. I think the emphasis is off videos—which is great—and it's returning back to stage, to interaction between the audience and the artist. It's entirely physical and dangerous at the moment, but I think artists and audiences are coming together again in a different way. Video was very much in the way between the artist and the audience over the last few years.

LODER: Which is your favorite new band?

BOWIE: The Screaming Blue Messiahs. I love them. I think they're terrific. . . . And I've always had a penchant for the Psychedelic Furs. I think they're a great band. I've always wanted to produce them, and they've often asked me to, but I never had the time. I would never be forward enough with most bands to suggest producing them, because I always like what it is they have themselves. It would never occur to me to suggest to, say, the Messiahs that I want to get involved with them. Because they seem to be so right on course with what they're doing that they need me like a hole in the head.

LODER: Does your son turn you on to groups?

BOWIE: Yeah. I got this band I've got to listen to, called the Stupids. I never heard of them. It's a band in England that Joe quite likes. He really liked PiL, until he saw them, which was unfortunate. I thought the last album was great, but we went to a bad show. The whole thing was so tired. There was no enthusiasm in the band or the audience . . .

I don't like many of the English bands at the moment. And the older ones, who *were* exciting, like the Fall . . . I mean, that new album by the Fall is such rubbish, such fourth-form poetry. It's really sophomoric.

LODER: Your own latest album has a certain recherché feel to it, with sitars and Mellotron, even some harmonica. And on one song, "Glass Spider," the backing vocal sounds remarkably like John Lennon.

BOWIE: Well, actually, the album *was* reflective in a way, because it covers every style that I've ever written in, I think. And also all the influences I've had in rock. On one song, "Zeroes," I wanted to put in every cliché that was around in the Sixties— "letting the love in," those kinds of lines. But it was done with affection—it's not supposed to be a snipe. I just wanted the feeling of that particular period, the very late Sixties.

LODER: What inspired the title track, "Never Let Me Down"?

BOWIE: It's basically about Coco, more than anybody else.

LODER: Is there a romantic relationship there?

BOWIE: No, it's platonic. But there is a romance in it, I guess, inasmuch as it's hard for two people to feel totally at ease in each other's company for that period of time and not expect too much from each other. Always being prepared to be there if the other one needs someone, you know? There's not many people you find in life that you can do that with, or feel that way with.

LODER: Any other long-term friendships?

BOWIE: Yeah, I've got three or four friends that I used to go to school with. One of them I've known since I was five.

I see them every year. In fact, we all came together again when I was forty—'cause they're all gonna be forty, too, you see. So we all met, and we just went back: "Oh, do you remember . . . ?" And "Did you ever think . . . ?" It was really something.

LODER: Do you think you've changed a lot over the years?

BOWIE: I'm more like I was in 1967 now, say, than I was in 1977. I *feel* like I am, anyway. I feel as bright and cheerful and optimistic as I was then—as opposed to feeling as depressed and sort of nihilistic as I was in the Seventies. I feel like I've come full circle in that particular way.

LODER: Well, you don't wear dresses anymore.

BOWIE: Do you know, the only time I wore dresses . . . There was that funny little white thing with white boots, which was Kansai's answer to Dick Whittington, if I remember: "It-a Dick-a Whittington-a!" "I see." "Sorta like-a international-a pantomime." "It's a dress, Kansai." "No, no—it's got-a boots." "Yeah—they're *satin* . . . All right, we'll do it."

And I did three drags for the "Boys Keep Swinging" video. And I wore a dress on *Saturday Night Live*, which was based on a John Heartfield photo montage—sort of a Communist Chinese air-hostess look. But I never wore dresses as much as Milton Berle did.

LODER: Do you feel relieved that you don't have the sort of burden of outrageousness on you anymore?

BOWIE: Why, no, not really. It's a bit of a disappointment. [*Laughs*] I'll keep tryin'. I've got a few things up me sleeve.

LODER: Any final fashion statement?

BOWIE: Wide shoulders are the flared trousers of the Eighties.

BOWIE AT THE BIJOU

INTERVIEW WITH VIRGINIA CAMPBELL
MOVIELINE
APRIL 1, 1992

Gee honey, how 'bout if we go see the new David Bowie movie?

If you've never uttered these words, you might not be the only one. It's possible nobody has. Maybe back in 1976, when Bowie, still cresting with the triumph of his album *Young Americans*, made his film debut in Nicolas Roeg's *The Man Who Fell to Earth*, some platform-shoed hipster laid out an extra line for his significant other and they raced together to the nearest theater.

But Roeg's unusual film so thoroughly confounded this groundswell that Bowie did not instantly become a Sinatra-like music-to-film crossover, which is what he himself said at the time that he intended to do. Nor did he correct his trajectory with his next film project, *Just a Gigolo*, which crawled belatedly on and quickly off screens in 1979. He had two big projects in 1983, Tony Scott's *The Hunger* and Nagisa Oshima's *Merry Christmas, Mr. Lawrence*, and both failed at the box office. By the time the Muppet epic *Labyrinth*, in which he starred as a goblin king, disappointed in 1986, Bowie was limiting his screen ambitions to cameos—in John

Landis's *Into the Night* in 1985, in Julien Temple's *Absolute Be-ginners* in 1986, and in Martin Scorsese's *The Last Temptation of Christ* in 1988.

Why, then, you might ask, is David Bowie on the cover of *Movieline*? Reasons could be cited. The long-delayed "quirky comedy" *The Linguini Incident*, in which Bowie stars opposite Rosanna Arquette and Buck Henry, is due out any day now. Also, Bowie has just done a cameo in David Lynch's upcoming *Twin Peaks: Fire Walk with Me*, and he is now in production on his directorial debut, a small, European-financed, as-yet-untitled film he wrote the script for. But those are pretexts. The truth is this: We like David Bowie. We like his movies. We don't care that none of his films has ever made any money. We think his work is at least as interesting as that of most of the dozen or so movie stars who might have been on our cover this month. And as a person, he's much more interesting.

Ziggy Stardust taught the Spiders from Mars to play twenty years ago. That's when David Bowie's daring, self-absorbed walk on the wild side really began to pick up speed. As Ziggy, he stylishly trampled such sacred notions of the day as "all you need is love." Ziggy didn't like hippies. He (cor-rectly) thought they'd gotten boring with their lazy, stoned-out embrace of the great amorphous values like peace, love, and understanding. All that "genuine" feeling was lousy showbiz. What about ungenuine feeling, the kind that made up most of everyone's internal life? The whole scene needed spiffing up, and Bowie was a one-man spiff-up squad. A little makeup, some orange hair dye, a taste of bisexuality and—this was the important part—a jolt of rock and roll so good and various and un-mellow it made the '70s bearable. Against the stupefying '60s ethos of "just be yourself," Bowie's music and behavior raised the useful question, "Which self?" He had quite a few. So did everybody else. It all got pretty crazy.

Looking back none too fondly on Bowie's heyday, music critic Stephen Fried wrote a couple of years ago that "Bowie was the first to recklessly fuck with the free world's head in a big theatrical way, not just focusing all kinds of adolescent cross-lust, but also mass marketing alienation and sexual weirdness." Well, for one thing, what's the free world good for if not to get its head fucked with once in a while? For another, Fried must have had some dull friends back then if they needed any help from David Bowie in getting alienated and weird.

But that is not to underestimate the extreme, authentic strangeness of David Bowie. There are reasons his stage and film roles have not included George in *Our Town* and have included: a space visitor, a gigolo, a vampire, a martyr, the Elephant Man, an evil advertising man, the guy who killed Christ, etc. These reasons go beyond his Boy Dietrich look and Daliesque anorexia. Bowie has always had a lot of theater going on behind the curtain of his earthy, unearthly flesh. The life of excess he so egregiously pursued in the '70s pumped up the volume. How insane was the lad? Of all the facts and fantasies I read about Bowie—and there are some sleazy, mean-spirited, badly researched, fascinating books out there—my single favorite outrageous, scarcely believable pseudo-factoid about his bad days was that during a stint in L.A. in 1975, he was so flipped out and paranoid on cocaine that he allegedly had a witch exorcize his house of demons (that's not the weird part) and then (this is the weird part) took to preserving his bodily fluids in jars in the refrigerator. The ultimate discouragement to midnight snacking. This I've got to ask him about. He probably won't even remember if he ever did such a thing—it was long ago, he's proper these days—but I've got to ask.

Maybe I won't ask. Nobody who at any time in the last twenty years preserved his bodily fluids in jars in the refrigerator would ever set 8:30 a.m. for an interview time. Rock stars across the city are just now shooing away their wasted groupies and passing out in disheveled suites. In the small, elegant living room of the small, elegant Manhattan hotel he is staying in, Bowie is already watching TV, the recap of a boxing match he seems to care about. He savors a few last punches, then turns the sound down to zero but leaves the picture on across the room over my shoulder as he gathers up a cup of coffee. Maneuvering around the period furniture in T-shirt, gym pants, and laceless hightops, Bowie is the most aerodynamic person I've ever seen up close. He looks designed to swoop where others have not swooped, and not to show up on radar.

I take out my tape recorder, a few pages of notes, and a book of poems I've brought as a present. "I don't know if you know this poet," I say. "He's wonderful but he's not really that well known, which is kind of amazing—being a well-kept secret for twenty years in the age of celebrity isn't easy." Bowie smiles, thanks me, checks out the book, which he has indeed heard of, and says, "Well, I've been a well-kept secret for twenty years. You've only seen the tip of the iceberg." There is not a trace of irony in his voice. It is the voice of a movie star, a voice John Garfield would have killed for, low, edged with a soft rasp that makes you listen. What I hear is a man who is not kidding, but is not dead serious either. A man who is just being a little playful first thing in the morning. The Diamond Dog is throwing the ball for me.

The night before flying to New York, I watched Bowie's brief performance as a serene, pragmatic Pontius Pilate in Martin Scorsese's *The Last Temptation of Christ*. "That's a strange movie to watch before going on a plane flight," Bowie laughs. "It's like, shall we find out—is there a God?" Then, as if moving on to the next logical topic, Bowie says, "I can't wait to see the other 10 percent of the Dead Sea Scrolls. They're in fragments, of course, kind of a Bill Burroughs effect . . ." and he recounts for me a certain conspiracy theory ("a '70s thing") about a secret section of the Dead Sea Scrolls supposedly written by a Jesus who'd escaped from the cross and ended up dying a revolutionary at Masada. This secret stuff is, according to the theory, held in the Vatican and shown only to each new Pope on the day of election. But what on earth, I ask, could the big secret be anyway? "Oh," laughs Bowie, "that there really was a Brian."

And that's about as serious as Bowie seems to want to get about his Scorsese film. "I had a great problem with the idiosyncratic accents. I fell afoul of that right at the beginning. It was kind of hard being there in Morocco with all these Method actors saying"—Bowie shifts into Brook-lynese—"'If we ged anutha plate o' coozcooz I'm gunna throwwhup! Fuck! Fuck you!!' And then the next day in character saying, 'So whadyaa get when ya look in da eyes uf an ant?' It was unreal. I kept cracking up." However amused by the proceedings,

Bowie managed a riveting, low-key scene with the Method Jesus in which, as Pilate, he sends his surreal white horse out of frame to neigh in the distance as he quietly condemns the Savior. "I was always told two things," he says. "Never work with animals and never work with Nicolas Roeg. I was waiting for the horse to take a dump on my big scene. But he was a good horse." And Bowie was a good Pilate.

"It seemed to me that the lower echelon of the bureaucracy of Rome was probably pretty similar to the British colonials who had to govern bits of Africa and India. It's sort of . . ." Bowie shifts precisely into his Pilate voice. "'Look, you people are causing too much trouble. I've got far too much work on my hands and I'm having a lot of complaints from Rome. We're going to bring you education, you'll have roads, but it all takes time. Let's just try to keep the system working—I do have the power to come to an ultimate conclusion about you chaps. For God's sake, I could have you crucified.' That's the part of the speech I thought was humorous."

Bowie is friendly enough with Scorsese to have been given a copy of Marty's storyboards from the big *Raging Bull* fight sequence ("The picture is, of course, in black and white, but in the storyboards the blood is painted in red"), but as a man who has himself put out good and bad product, he calls a spade a spade: "I hated *Cape Fear*. I was so disappointed. It felt like he was bored, like he was playing with the camera instead of getting into the thing. The story is sublimely silly. It was all making a silk purse out of a sow's ear. There was one series of shots I couldn't believe, five zoom-ins in a row, and I thought, I don't know whether he's saying, 'You'll buy this, sucker,' or 'I don't like what I'm doing.' It was a message in a lens."

Bowie's part in *Temptation* was exactly one scene, in keeping with his apparent strategy of doing cameos for directors who interest him instead of doing possibly grander roles for directors who don't. With the exception of first-time director Richard Shepard's *The Linguini Incident*, which, Bowie explains, he did because the starring role as a bartender was one in which "I could just be me," Bowie says that "on any project, I take into consideration first, foremost, above the storyline, above the role, who is directing. Is it somebody I'd like to observe firsthand?" In the case of David Lynch, yes. Bowie spent two days on Lynch's *Fire Walk with Me* (the movie prequel to the TV *Twin Peaks*) last year, playing an FBI agent who reappears, after long being presumed dead, to drop some clues about Laura Palmer's predicament. I ask Bowie what his favorite Lynch movie is. "Oh, I'm afraid it would be *Eraserhead*. I think it's an adorable film, quite lovely. It's such a pure form of his enthusiasm for making films. I think he's veered off now, but I saw him initially as much more of a painterly filmmaker."

"A lot of people seem to think Lynch has gone off the deep end," I remark.

"If you put his work alongside what Europe's been producing for the last fifty years, it's not so wacky. It's all relative. People would think Lynch has gone nuts if they've been brought up on Tony Scott, yes. But crikey. One good sharp dose of *Un Chien Andalou* would set them straight."

"I'm talking about people who know *Un Chien Andalou*. They just think Lynch has lost control."

"They want that. They'd love that, wouldn't they? People are always looking for chinks in the armor in this business."

Realizing he has just uttered a cliché, a sin he does not easily allow himself, Bowie leans forward and adopts the tone of a cigar-chomping showbiz know-it-all. "Ya know, in this business, Virginia . . ."

"I read the synopsis of *Fire Walk with Me* and I couldn't tell what the hell it was about."

"You wait," says Bowie, now shifting into mock-hype mode. "You ain't seen nuthin' yet, baby. I read his script to *Ronnie Rocket* [a long-planned Lynch project]. I have never, in my entire life—wait, how can I be really glib—" He gathers himself up and pronounces with TV movie critic blurb relish that "*Ronnie Rocket* makes *Eraserhead* look like *Dallas*."

"I wanted to see if Lynch was quite as cerebral as everybody had always told me he was," Bowie continues. "He is. But he's quite scattered. On the set he's quite alarmingly nuts. He was super. Working with him was probably very much what it was like working with Nic Roeg—if I remembered."

The key year in Bowie's film karma was 1975, when wild rock and roll success was finally his. He was living in L.A., showbiz Mission Control, where offers of every kind were being hurled his way. And so a rough year it was. Cameron Crowe, now a film director but then an intrepid journalist, caught the spirit of these fast times in a now justly famous *Playboy* interview based on his travels with a uniquely unleashed Bowie, a Bowie who had given up conventional sleep patterns and, one surmises, was fueling his revelations about such things as his bisexuality (which he has since disavowed) and his taste for fascism (which he has since disavowed) with large quantities of cocaine. ("It's kind of good, isn't it?" Bowie says with a low, clenched-jaw laugh at the mention of this past bit of public relations.)

"Weren't you considering doing a movie version of *Stranger in a Strange Land* back in 1975?"

"No, I was offered it many, many times by many, many different producers. I absolutely never had any intention of doing it. It was a staggeringly, awesomely trite book." The film Bowie did decide to do was based on another science fiction book he describes as "quite a pallid little story," *The Man Who Fell to Earth*. Both stories are about space aliens, but the latter project was to be directed by Nicolas Roeg, the man who'd done well by Mick Jagger in Performance and could be counted on to transform the pallid into the perplexing. Roeg, having gotten over his notion of having a too-old Peter O'Toole play The Man, no doubt knew of Bowie's rock-life self-casting as a non-Earthling, but probably considered that incidental. He may well have seen more in Bowie back then than Bowie did, which is saying something.

"Roeg phoned my office in New York and made an appointment to see me," Bowie recalls, "and I turned up a day late. He came at four o'clock on a Saturday afternoon and I went out all night because I was doing my drug of choice and I got back midday the next day and he'd stayed overnight in my kitchen waiting. He won me over just by that. I was being very snobby about making films—you know, 'I'm not sure I want to do your little movie.' I had plans of taking over show business. This film really didn't fit into my scheme of things. I read bits of the script, as much as I was able to at the time, thirty seconds at a go."

The Man Who Fell to Earth turned out to be an inspired,

irreducible piece about an alien who comes to earth to rescue
his own planet from drought through an elaborate, doomed
plan involving the development of a Howard Hughes–ish
empire. Bowie, ethereal almost to the point of transpar-
ency, was brilliant casting as the Visitor who, Roeg wanted
us to understand, comes as much from metaphorical inner
as literal outer space. While Roeg's achievement flew by
most critics (who never do seem to do the right drugs),
Bowie caught them all off guard and won their praise. This
bizarre-looking rock creature of dubious sexual identity
could act.

Bowie claims he wasn't acting: "I just threw my real self
into that movie as I was at that time. It was the first thing I'd
ever done. I was virtually ignorant of the established proce-
dure, so I was going a lot on instinct, and my instinct was
pretty dissipated. I just learned the lines for that day and did
them the way I was feeling. It wasn't that far off. I actually
was feeling as alienated as that character was. It was a pretty
natural performance. What you see there is David Bowie."

"Well, it's an awfully good performance."

"It's a good exhibition—of somebody literally falling
apart in front of you. I was totally insecure with about ten
grams a day in me. I was stoned out of my mind from beginning to end."

Ten grams a day? That's Hiroshima plus Nagasaki. I'd
have been putting my bodily fluids in the refrigerator too.
Bowie lights his fifth or sixth Marlboro in the ongoing, theo-
retically milder assault on his longevity that he allows himself
these days and explains, "I was out of my head from '74 till at
least through '76, in a serious and dangerous manner."

"Was Roeg ever bothered by your being so out of it on his set?"

"I don't remember him ever getting angry with me. We got on rather well. I think I was fulfilling what he needed from me for that role. I wasn't disrupting . . . I wasn't disrupted. In fact, I was very eager to please. And amazingly enough, I was able to carry out everything I was asked to do. I was quite willing to stay up as long as anybody. I'd go home and stay up even then, and write and make albums and do all this stuff all the time. Days on end. I've got thousands of paintings."

Oil or acrylic? Bowie laughs. "Acrylic! It's fast. Bzzzzzzzzzzzzz. Done. Next!" Perhaps because Bowie's love of the nonlinear is catching, I suddenly want to know what he thinks of Willem de Kooning's latest work, the paintings done since the maestro got senile and quit talking. Truth is, I can picture Bowie ending up like this at 90 or 100.

"I actually visited de Kooning."

"What state was he in?"

"Fake catatonic, I think. I went with some friends and I think he just didn't want visitors. As we walked in, he was painting . . ." Bowie gets up and stands crouched with an invisible, unmoving brush poised at the surface of an invisible canvas, "very much like that. And then he made a big number of sitting in his rocking chair and we got three words out of him the whole time. He sat there waiting—'Oh fuck, visitors'—then he wanted us to realize we'd disrupted his day because he didn't wait for us to go. As we were walking out, he got back up and started painting again. There's a man who's aware of the existence of life and death at the same time."

The phone rings and Bowie crosses the room to answer

it. He speaks very briefly in a soft voice to his publicist, who is asking how things are going and letting him know the schedule for getting to his performance by evening in another city. It's all very calm, very '90s. "I had a very strange offer the other night I must tell you about," he says as he sits back down and refocuses. Because of a much discussed peculiarity of his eyes—one of his irises is paralyzed from a childhood fight—Bowie tends to focus your attention when he's focusing his. "Someone sent me a *Mormon Bible* and five hundred dollars in cash to have a couple of hours to spend with me." He laughs lightly at this, marveling. "Of course, I returned both. I think a straightforward presentation of the *Mormon Bible* and a request to maybe have a chat about it might have produced a different result. It was the inclusion of the five hundred dollars I felt was particularly weird. Buying my time. Really odd."

Since Bowie has struck so many poses throughout his professional life, quite a few of them overtly borrowed from some of the great pose-strikers of all time, one assumes he carried out a study of past masters at some point. He bristles at the suggestion: "I never was consumed by star stuff, even slightly. If ever there was anything I would redirect about how people have thought about me it's that I must have had an obsession or deep empathy with people like Garbo or Dietrich—that star element, that mystique. It never at any time had anything to do with what I was trying to do. It was inadvertent. My main preoccupation throughout everything I've ever done has been the concept of what I was writing about. And the problem of how it should be presented was the priority. It was never 'I want to be alone,' or any of that shit."

As far as, say, the obvious Garbo/Dietrich look on the cover of the *Changesonebowie* album, "It was just a matter of trying to get an interesting album cover. I never lived up to that look. I was never like that." Nevertheless, in past interviews Bowie himself used to talk about James Dean being an influence. "I wonder if he was," he says to me now, as if we are discussing someone else's life. "There were aspects of him . . . I wasn't crazy about his acting. I thought he was an interesting actor, but not brilliant. I'm much more persuaded by the acting of Montgomery Clift, truly one of the most brilliant presences on celluloid. I thought Dean had some great gimmicks. He knew how to eat up a camera, but I don't think it had much to do with acting. He was over-greedy in his performances. What I had empathy with were the simple things. His alleged bisexuality interested me at the time. The ways he conducted himself with people were probably very much like I was, in an Anglo fashion. The same kind of dysfunctional behavior I recognized and was drawn to."

And speaking of dysfunctional behavior, Bowie once described the movie he made after *The Man Who Fell to Earth* as "all of Elvis's thirty-two movies rolled into one." Actually, it's not quite that good. Directed by David Hemmings, *Just a Gigolo* was the project that Bowie, having departed from the insanity of Los Angeles without totally regaining his senses in Berlin, where he'd gone to live, signed on to do with the following cast: Marlene Dietrich, Kim Novak, Maria Schell, Curt Jurgens, Hemmings, and one Sydne Rome. Regrettably, Ms. Rome, unknown then and destined to remain so, had the largest role opposite Bowie's gigolo. Dietrich, looking a lot like Myrna Loy did on the Oscars last year, had only a cameo. Novak, looking a little like Myrna Loy on the Oscars, had a somewhat larger role, dancing a tango in a ghastly raspberry dress with her nipples highly visible. Bowie, who, this film proves conclusively, cannot embarrass himself on film, is merely badly lit. "I'm such a control freak that I would like to buy *Gigolo* back—this is a pipe dream of mine—and redo the entire thing. It actually read very well. If only Hemmings had applied himself. But David was too fond, like myself at the time, of having a good time. The second day, we looked at each other and said, 'God, this is a piece of shit. Let's have a good time.' We were just having a lark for seven weeks."

A little less fun and Bowie's life in the cinema might have gone differently. But after a searing decade of show business that had included speedy transitions from one stage persona to the next, Bowie was in retreat. Though he made great music at that time, he was not up to the next logical step as far as his film career was concerned: following his critically well-received performance in *The Man Who Fell to Earth* with a film that did well at the box office. Besides *Gigolo*, he did no film work at all for the next few years. He did, however, star on Broadway in *The Elephant Man*, and elicited acclaim that respectfully ignored his stature as rock star. Not until 1983 did he appear onscreen again, this time in two films. One, *Merry Christmas, Mr. Lawrence*, directed by the extremely Japanese Nagisa Oshima, had Bowie cast as a prisoner in a Japanese World War II POW camp in Java. "I think Oshima had an enormous problem understanding the Western thought process," says Bowie, responding to the adjective I say a friend of mine used to describe the film: "dotty." "With his Japanese actors he was very severe, down to the minutest detail. With

Tom Conti and me, he said, 'Please do whatever it is you people do.'"

In a story that could have used a lot more of him and a lot less of everybody else, including the Japanese soldier who commits interminable hara-kiri onscreen, Bowie had one especially remarkable scene where his character, Celliers, thinking he's about to be executed, performs a mime of shaving, smoking, and drinking tea, as if savoring the last precious moments of life. "Yes, well, that's what I was thinking—I'm not going to waste this precious moment," Bowie laughs. "Oshima just gave that scene to me with no direction." Later Celliers dies a martyr's death, buried up to his neck in sand. "Oshima just said, 'Now, we going to bury you up to your head!' I had to cope and find something in me—though, believe me, it was very easy to understand what it felt like to be buried up to my head."

The other '83 venture was a film that now enjoys something of a cult status, *The Hunger*, in which Bowie, playing the vampire consort of Catherine Deneuve, suddenly begins aging rapidly and, unable to be helped by gerontologist Susan Sarandon, ends up a heap of sentient dust—no doubt a bracing acting exercise for a well-over-thirty rock star. Directed by British import Tony Scott (only in Hollywood could a guy direct both Bruce Willis and David Bowie in the same decade), the film is actually a snazzily accurate depiction of modern addiction, not the glitzily stupid vampire shtick it was accused of being when it was released. Bowie, who even now looks like he lives on chicken bullion, was fully convincing as a vampire with tragic needs.

"First let me say," Bowie begins, "that Sarandon is one

of the brightest, wittiest, bestest actors I've ever worked with. Also, as a person, she's delightful and intelligent. Let me say that, because I've never actually been asked . . ." I must be looking at him a little blankly, because he leans into the tape recorder, "and I wasn't asked just now! Anyway, I think she's fantastic." Bowie clears his throat. "Tony Scott had one particular vision of this movie. The script Tony, Susan, and I talked about was different from the sensibility of the actual film. He had no power at all and had to bow to demands. I have every respect that he kept his cool throughout the whole proceedings and actually got the film finished. Let's say that it was a case of 'More blood!!!' Tony was trying to pull back from such situations and treat things in a more psychological manner. And this is Tony Scott we're talking about. Believe it or not, it was a very intelligent look at the subject. And now he's known for having a less than three-dimensional look at life. I don't think he's made a Tony Scott film yet. I saw him walk away from *The Hunger* shattered. I think he came away with a completely different idea of what filmmaking was about in America, or with American money."

So, perhaps, did Bowie. Apart from his sly turn as a goblin king in *Labyrinth*, a film children now watch fanatically on video ("Every Christmas," says Bowie, "a new flock of children comes up to me and says, 'Oh! you're the one who's in *Labyrinth*!'"), it's been cameos only since then. In qualitative terms, of course, Bowie has fared better than any other rock star onscreen. Prince, Madonna, Elvis, and the rest are cinematic fingernails-on-chalkboard. Bowie alone has been as much an actor as a rock star from the start.

"I think if you didn't know that Jagger was Jagger," Bowie

tells me, countering my opinion about rockers onscreen, "and of course that baggage comes with us, but if you just looked at Performance objectively, you'd see an extraordinarily interesting actor."

"But then again, if you looked at Ned Kelly . . ."

"I didn't say that film. I wasn't going to breathe a word about it."

I suggest that we can just wait and see with Jagger's *Freejack*. "I turned that film down," says Bowie. When I tell Bowie I bet he's turned down some awful stuff, he shrugs and goes "Pffffff" with a mixture of horror and disdain. "You wouldn't believe it. There've been a few where I said, 'Shit, I wish I could've done that.' But there've been more . . ." Like what, besides the occasional Bond villain? "Like Ford Fairlane. The Wayne Newton part." Yikes. "I was offered a part in Kafka, a part someone could have done something with. But the script itself made no sense. I thought, why are they making this film? What are you saying about Kafka that makes any sense?"

A rumor a few years back had Bowie and Jagger as the original stars for *Mountains of the Moon*. "I was offered *Mountains of the Moon* separately, before Mick. He and I were interested in doing a film together, though. There was one written for us, but it never got to us and became that Michael Caine–Steve Martin movie *Dirty Rotten Scoundrels*. How 'bout them apples! Mick and I were a bit tweezed that we lost out on a script that could have been reasonably good. But *Mountains* with Mick? It figures slimly in my memory. When we were much younger—and that, my dear, was many years ago, when there were mountains on the moon, when we lived in the mountains on the moon—it was bandied around that we should play Byron and Shelley. I think we were stupid never to have done it. But we weren't very serious about anything in those days. Maybe as older men we'll do Pinter, in our seventies"—Bowie broadens his accent for effect—"on the Broadway stage!"

At least Bowie and Jagger didn't get involved in Ken Russell's treatment of the Romantic poets, or in any other Russell film, for that matter. "I wouldn't even dream of it. I can't stand his movies. There isn't even one I like." One of the films Bowie did dream of doing was *At Play in the Fields of the Lord.* "I would have given my right arm to play the role of the missionary. But not with that director [Hector Babenco]. Richard Gere and I both wanted to do this film. He wanted to play the Indian pilot and was fighting to get the rights. It was all far too complicated, and, anyway, we lost it. Had it been resolved in a different way, it would have been a glorious film to participate in."

I ask Bowie how committed he is to film acting at this point. "Not very," he shoots back. Directing is another matter. Having recently sent up the profession with his very funny portrayal of the vicious, imperious British director Sir Roland Moorcock in a John Landis–directed episode of HBO's *Dream On*, Bowie is actually going behind the camera in real life. Over the last two years he has written a script and he's now in production on it. "It's not going to be a special effects movie."

"I would never have thought that—"

"Quite. But that's what people ask me. It's a performance piece with four actors, basically. There's a larger cast, but that's the pivotal plot. I think, immodestly, it would have more to

owe to Cassavetes than Spielberg. It's about personalities, and
the destructive effect of one person's challenge and control
over another person's life. It doesn't matter what they are—
they could be dentists. The story takes place in L.A. I know
the good and bad sides of that town, after a period of close
on eighteen years. I can almost read L.A. like a person, its at-
tributes and characteristics. So, L.A. itself would be the fifth
performance."

I tell Bowie that a friend of mine recently remarked to
me that the amazing thing about L.A. is that all the clichés
about it are absolutely true. He smiles. "You know, Dame
Edith Evans went to Los Angeles in the '60s, and she was
given a tour through Hollywood, and after a week she was
asked what was singularly the most interesting thing she'd
seen there. And she said, 'Well, one day I went to Griffith
Observatory and the director took me down to the basement,
down through a corridor that was very badly lit, at the end
of which was a refrigerator. He opened the refrigerator and
took out two pieces of glass, and between the two pieces of
glass was a snowflake that fell upon Los Angeles in 1935. That
was the most interesting thing I saw in Los Angeles.'" Bowie
smiles. "Nic Roeg told me that story."

Writing a screenplay, Bowie says, "is not like writing a
song at all. It's not like writing anything but a screenplay. It's
stunningly hard. The first thirty-five pages were fun. Then I
hit a wall." The visual part of directing doesn't bother him.
The rest does. "I'm a ball of sweat when I think about what
I have to do; it really is terrifying," he says, simulating self-
strangulation. "I'm being secretive about this because I want
the film to come out without any expectations whatsoever."

Directing is a longtime desire of Bowie's. As early as the fateful 1975, when he either did or did not take to preserving his bodily fluids in the refrigerator, he had a project he was ready to proceed with. "Thank God, I never did. First, I don't think I would have had the discipline to put it all together properly. I would have been in one of those dreadful situations where money was being poured down the drain. I don't think I'd have had the psychological stamina to keep it together. Now I feel I can at least accomplish the task, and hopefully with some degree of elegance. But back in '75, I got near to doing the most alarming piece. Very strange and satanic. Based on the Antichrist. I wrote it myself during about seven of those sleepless nights. Complete with drawings and character studies. There was an unbelievable postapocalyptic nihilism to the kids in it, some of whom I'd borrowed from *Diamond Dogs*—I remember vast gangs of boys on these huge rollerskates that were rusted and squeaked. There were elements not dissimilar to what would become *Mad Max*—I later came out of that film thinking they must have seen my project. I was," Bowie says drolly, "unaware of synchronicity. Anyway, the Jesus figure, which I took from the idea of the Jesus scrolls, was a freedom fighter instead of the King of Mankind. Terence Stamp was cast in my mind as Jesus, and I had a younger kid, who was unbelievably like the kid who would soon become John Lydon of the Sex Pistols, cast as Jesus's son. It was all very pre-punk. The very last scene was Jesus being rowed out to a ship that was like a Fritz Lang *Titanic* by a hooded figure whose cloak gets pulled up as he's rowing and Jesus sees the goat hooves. It's a wonderful read. John Lennon looked over it and said, 'Why the fuck do you want to make this?? This is so fucking evil!' And I said, 'But it's going to look great!'"

The refrigerator story is beginning to gain some credibility with me again, but I can't yet bring myself to ask about it. Instead I ask Bowie how fixated he was on movies as a kid. "Not at all. I quite liked television when I was a kid. Movies not till much later. Then I'd sneak off from being a rock god and watch art movies. I could hire movies from the Met in New York—this was real early in the '70s—and I had a reel-to-reel video player, one of the first. You could show these movies on a white wall and film them off the wall. So I started this collection of German Expressionist movies. Of course," Bowie says, leaning in to speak into the tape recorder, "I don't have them any more. I had everything. Murnau, Pabst, Lang. I went crazy and lived in that world for about a year, and it had a lot to do with what I was doing in rock."

This reminds Bowie of a Giorgio Moroder story ("You know who he is—the guy who put the fascist marching beat behind Donna Summer?"): "One of the harebrained schemes I had for a long time was to take *Metropolis* and put a soundtrack on it written by Brian Eno and me. I wanted to get a pristine print and have live parts enacted on stage in front of the screen. I thought it such a novel idea that nobody else was going to buy the rights just now. So I was working with Moroder on the music for 'Cat People.' I love Moroder. This is Moroder: He says to Paul Schrader, 'I want my apartment to look just like that wonderful apartment in American *Gigolo*,' and Schrader says, 'Yes, of course, I'm sure you can get it done just like Richard's apartment,' and Giorgio says, 'No, not that apartment, the pimp's apartment!' So,

I'm working with Giorgio and he says, 'Did you see *Napoleon*? I thought it was stunning, and I knew I could do something like that—put some music to an old movie.' And I was going, 'Yeah . . .' And he said, 'I've found the film! Nobody's ever heard of it! It's *Metropolis*, and I've bought the rights!'" Bowie groans with deadpan mirth. "I didn't even tell him. It ruined my week. He played me some of the stuff he'd written, and it was like—" Bowie does a disco beat and sings, "'I'm the master, you're the slave.'" He breaks up laughing.

Bowie's publicist has returned by now, and she tells him he has to finish up. He graciously acknowledges her orders in a beautifully enacted reversal of the actual hierarchy. As I'm gathering my things to leave, Bowie looks across the room at the TV silently flickering with a football game. "Ha! I love it when they bang their helmets together like that—you know, when something good happens—like a high-five sign!" I suddenly realize I haven't asked the refrigerator question. But how does one begin to ask such an outrageous question, anyway? "You know, people always talk about your manipulation of your image and all of that, much of which is of course true, but no one really talks about how playful you are . . ." Bowie, standing up for the goodbye, says, "I do wonder when I see these things that come off as if I'm so po-faced or something." I'm already at the door. It's too late to ask my question now. I'll just have to write it off as a disappointing failure of nerve. I thank the man and leave.

Moments later, in the lobby of Bowie's hotel, I do a mental check to see that I have everything with me. Coat, purse, tape recorder . . . my notes. I left my notes on the coffee table. Who cares, I tell myself quickly. The maid will throw them away, I don't need them now. No. I do need them. Not only that, in those notes, carefully scripted to prevent a failure of nerve, is the question about the jars of bodily fluids. The tiniest possibility that Bowie would pick up the notes—to scribble down a phone number, whatever—and read that question, even if I never hear about it, drives me crazy. Masking my unease, I ask the publicist if we can go back up and get the notes. She kindly agrees to call up to the room. When we knock at Bowie's door, he opens it. In his hand are the notes, neatly folded, just as I left them. He looks at me with a fantastic, diabolical twinkle in his eye, holds them out and says, "You'll never know."

FASHION: TURN TO THE LEFT FASHION: TURN TO THE RIGHT

CONVERSATION WITH ALEXANDER McQUEEN
DAZED AND CONFUSED
NOVEMBER 1996

This conversation took place on the phone, as is always the case with my conversations with Alex. We have worked together for over a year on various projects and never once met. It's a beautiful Sunday afternoon and he is in the verdant green hills of Gloucestershire visiting at the house of his friend, Isabella Blow. Ringring. Ringring. Ringring.

• • •

BOWIE: Are you gay and do you take drugs? [*Laughter*]

McQUEEN: Yes, to both of them. [*More laughter*]

BOWIE: So what are your drugs of choice?

McQUEEN: A man called Charlie!

BOWIE: Do you find that it affects the way you approach your designing?

McQUEEN: Yeah, it makes it more erratic. That's why you get my head blown up shot. [In reference to a Nick Knight photograph at the Florence Biennale.]

BOWIE: Well, I once asked you to make me a specific jacket in a certain color and you sent me something entirely different in a tapestry fabric, quite beautiful I might add, but how would you cope in the more corporate world?

McQUEEN: I wouldn't be in a corporate world.

BOWIE: Even if you're going to be working for a rather large fashion house like Givenchy?

McQUEEN: Yeah.

BOWIE: So how are you going to work in these circumstances? Do you feel as though you're going to have rules and parameters placed on you, or what?

McQUEEN: Well, yeah, but you know I can only do it the way I do it. That's why they chose me and if they can't accept that, they'll have to get someone else. They're going to have no choice at the end of the day because I work to my own laws and requirements, not anyone else's. I sound a bit like yourself!

BOWIE: Armani or Versace?

McQUEEN: Marks and Spencer.

BOWIE: Unlike most designers, your sense of wear seems to derive from forms other than the fashion history. You take or steal quite arbitrarily from, say the neo-Catholic macabre photographs of Joel-Peter Witkin, to rave culture. Do you think fashion is art?

MCQUEEN: No, I don't. But I like to break down barriers. It's not a specific way of thinking, it's just what's in my mind at the time. It could be anything—it could be a man walking down the street or a nuclear bomb going off—it could be anything that triggers some sort of emotion in my mind. I mean, I see everything in a world of art in one way or another. How people do things. The way people kiss.

BOWIE: Who or what are your present influences?

MCQUEEN: Let me think. I don't know. I think that's a really hard question because in one way, one side of me is kind of really sombre and the other side of my brain is very erratic and it's always this fight against the other and I choose so many different things. This is why my shows always throw people completely: one minute I see a lovely chiffon dress and the next minute I see a girl in this cage that makes her walk like a puppet and, you know, they can't understand where it's coming from because there are so many sides of me in conflict. But influences are really from my own imagination and not many come from direct sources. They usually come from a lone force of say, the way I want to perform sex or the way I want people to perform sex or the way I want to see people act, or what would happen if a person was like that. You know what I mean? It's not from direct sources. It's just sort of from a big subconscious or the perverse. I don't think like the average person on the street. I think quite perversely sometimes in my own mind.

BOWIE: Yeah, I would say, from just looking at the way you work, that sexuality plays a very important part in the way that you design.

McQUEEN: Well, because I think it's the worst mental attitude. Sexuality in a person trying to define one's sexuality. Finding which way you sway or what shocks you in other people and who accepts you at the end of the day when you're looking for love. You have to go through these corridors and it can be kind of mind-blowing sometimes.

BOWIE: There's something a lot more pagan about your work compared, say, to Gaultier. Your things work at a more organic level.

McQUEEN: Possibly. I gather some influence from the Marquis de Sade because I actually think of him as a great philosopher and a man of his time, where people found him just a pervert. [*Laughs*] I find him sort of influential in the way he provokes people's thoughts. It kind of scares me. That's the way I think but, at the end of the day, that's the way my entity has grown and, all in all, in my life, it's the way I am.

BOWIE: Do you think of clothes themselves as being a way of torturing society?

McQUEEN: I don't put such an importance on clothes, anyway. I mean at the end of the day they are, after all, just clothes and I can't cure the world of illness with clothes. I just try to make the person that's wearing them feel more confident in themselves because I am so unconfident. I'm really insecure in a lot of ways and I suppose my confidence comes out in the clothes I design anyway. I'm very insecure as a person.

BOWIE: Aren't we all? Could you design a car?

McQUEEN: Could I? It would be as flat as an envelope if I designed a car.

BOWIE: Could you design a house?

McQUEEN: Yes, very easily, very easily.

BOWIE: Do you paint or sculpt?

McQUEEN: No. I buy sculptures. I don't do it, I buy it. I buy lots of sculptures.

BOWIE: Do you ever work in the visual arts?

McQUEEN: No, but I just did a show the other day. I don't know if you heard, but we did this show, it was on water and we did this kind of cocoon for this girl made of steel rods and it was in the form of a three-dimensional star and it was covered in this glass fabric so you could see through it and this girl was inside it, but we had all these butterflies flying around her inside it. So she was picking them out of the air and they were landing on her hand. It was just about the girl's own environment. So I was thinking about the new millennium in the future thinking you would carry around with you your home like a snail would. She was walking along in the water with a massive star covered in glass and the butterflies and death-faced moths were flying around her and landing on her hand and she was looking at them. It was really beautiful. It threw a lot of people completely sideways.

BOWIE: It's interesting how what you're talking about is somewhere between theatre and installation.

McQUEEN: Well, I hate the theatre, I hate it. I used to work in the theatre. I used to make costumes for them and films, and it's one thing I've always detested—the theatre. I hate going to the theatre, it bores me shitless.

BOWIE: Well, I'm not talking about a play.

McQUEEN: I know, but I just wanted to tell you that anyway! [*Laughs*]

BOWIE: All right, change the word to ritual.

McQUEEN: Yeah, that's better. I like ritual . . . [*Laughs*]

BOWIE: Armani says, "Fashion is dead."

McQUEEN: Oh, so is he . . . I mean, God . . .

BOWIE: Now you sound like Versace . . .

McQUEEN: He's close to dead. I mean, no one wants to wear a floppy suit in a nice wool—the man was a bloody window dresser. What does he know?

BOWIE: Do you think that what he's really saying is that maybe . . .

McQUEEN: He's lost it . . .

BOWIE: He might still be making an observation in as much as the boundaries are coming down . . .

McQUEEN: Yeah.

BOWIE: The way fashion is presented these days is a quantum leap from how it was presented say, five to ten years ago. It's become almost a new form, hasn't it?

McQUEEN: Yeah, but you know you can't depend on fashion designers to predict the future of society, you know, at the end of the day they're only clothes and that never strays from my mind for one minute.

BOWIE: Is the British renaissance a reality or a hype do you think? The world is being told that it's so. Through all strata of British life and from fashion to visual arts, music, obviously, architecture, I mean there's not one aspect of culture where Brits haven't got some pretty fair leaders, English designers in

French houses, you know what I mean? It's like we're pervading the whole zeitgeist at the moment.

McQUEEN: Being British yourself, I think you understand that Britain always led the way in every field possible in the world from art to pop music. Even from the days of Henry VIII. It's a nation where people come and gloat at what we have as a valuable heritage, be it some good, some bad, but there's no place like it on earth.

BOWIE: But why is it we can't follow through once we've initially created something? We're far better innovators than we are manufacturers.

McQUEEN: Yeah, exactly. But I think that's a good thing. I don't think that's a bad thing. It makes you holy, it makes you quite respectable about what you do and the actual money-making part of it is for the greedy.

BOWIE: So you're not greedy, Alex?

McQUEEN: I'm afraid I'm not. Money's never been a big object. Well, I mean I like to live comfortably, but I've been asked by this French fashion house how would I put on a show and I said, well, the sort of money these people buy these clothes for in this day and age, you don't want to flaunt your wealth in front of the average Joe Public because it's bad taste and with all the troubles in the world today, it's not a good thing to do anyway. I'm sure these people that have this sort of money don't feel like showing their face on camera, so

I said it would be more of a personal show and people with this sort of money who do appreciate good art and good quality clothes and have these one-off pieces made just respect the ideal, not the actual chucking money around. They can do that anywhere.

BOWIE: So when you are affluent, which I'm afraid is probably in the cards for you, how are you going to deal with that?

McQUEEN: I'd like to buy Le Corbusier's house in France . . . [*Sniggers*]

BOWIE: Here's a nice thing. What was the first thing you designed ever? Like when you were little or a kid or something?

McQUEEN: Oh. I can't think that far back, but for my own professional career, it was the bumsters. The ones that Gail, your bass player, wears.

BOWIE: Was there a point when you were sort of playing around with stuff, and when you used to dress up and go to clubs when you were a kid, and all that, where you would do original things?

McQUEEN: Actually, yeah. I would wear my sister's clothes and people wouldn't recognize it because I'd wear them in a male way. I did go round my street once in my sister's bra when I was about twelve years old and the neighbors thought I was a freaky kid, got dirty looks and all that . . . and you're talking about Stepney here.

BOWIE: My father used to work in Stepney.

McQUEEN: Yeah?

BOWIE: What age were you when you left home?

McQUEEN: Nineteen.

BOWIE: Did it give you an incredible feeling of freedom? Or did you suddenly feel even more vulnerable?

McQUEEN: I felt really vulnerable actually. Because I was the youngest and I was always mollycoddled by my mother, so that's why I turned out to be a fag, probably. [*Laughter*]

BOWIE: [*Laughing*] Was it a clear choice?

McQUEEN: I fancied boys when I went to Pontins at three years old!

BOWIE: Did you ever go on holiday to Butlins or Bognor Regis or Great Yarmouth?

McQUEEN: No, I went to Pontins in Camber Sands.

BOWIE: Camber Sands?! I used to go there too!

McQUEEN: Oh my God!

BOWIE: They had a trailer park with caravans . . .

McQUEEN: Exactly.

BOWIE: . . . and next door to us we had a, at the time, very well-known comedian, Arthur Haynes, who was sort of like a bit of a wide boy; that was his bit on stage, you know, and I used to go over and try and get his autograph. I went three mornings running and he told me to fuck off every day. [*Laughing*] That was my first time I met a celebrity and I was so let down. I felt if that's what it's all about . . . they're just real people.

McQUEEN: Two memories on Pontins—one was coming 'round the corner and seeing my two sisters getting off with two men. [*Laughter*] I thought they were getting raped and I went screaming back to my Mum and I wound up getting beat up by my two sisters! The other one was turning up in Pontins when we first got there and looking out the cab window 'cause my family was, like, full of cabbies; it was like a gypsy caravan–load to go to these places, and I looked out the window when I got there and there were these two men with these scary masked faces on and I shit myself there and then in the cab! I literally just shit my pants! [*Laughter*]

BOWIE: Which comes to . . . who is the shiftiest designer?

McQUEEN: Oh my God . . .

BOWIE: Who is the worst designer?

McQUEEN: In my eyes?

BOWIE: Yeah, in your eyes.

McQUEEN: Oh God, I'm open for libel here now, David . . .

BOWIE: Do you think there's more than one?

McQUEEN: I think you've got to blame the public that buy the clothes of these people, not the designers themselves, because it turns out they haven't got much idea about, you know, design itself. It's the people that buy the stuff. My favorite designer, though, is Rei Kawakubo. She's the only one I buy, the only clothes I buy ever for myself as a designer are Comme des Garçons. I spent about a thousand pounds last year (I shouldn't say that) on Comme des Garçons menswear . . .

BOWIE: I've never paid, Alex! [*Laughs*] Until . . .

McQUEEN: Until you met me! [*More laughter*]

BOWIE: Until I met you! Yes, but I knew that you needed it!

McQUEEN: I did at the time! But I tell you what I did do when you paid me, I paid the people that actually made the coat!

BOWIE: No, listen, you were so kind about the couple of things that I didn't need that you actually gave me. I thought that was very sweet of you. You work very well in a collaborative way as well. I thought the stuff . . .

McQUEEN: I still haven't bloody met you yet! [*Laughs*]

BOWIE: I know, I think it's quite extraordinary that we've done so well with the stage things that we put together. Do you enjoy collaboration?

McQUEEN: I do, but the one thing you have to do when you collaborate is actually respect the people that you work with: and people have phoned me up and asked me to collaborate with them before and I've usually turned them down.

BOWIE: Do your clients really know what they want and what is right for them, or do you usually have to dress them from the floor up?

McQUEEN: It can work either way and I don't resent either because, at the end of the day, I'm the clothes designer and they are the public. If you want a house built you're not expected to build it yourself.

BOWIE: Here's a fan question. Who would you like to dress more than anyone else in the world and why?

McQUEEN: There's no one I'd like to dress more than anyone else in the world, I'm afraid. I can't think of anyone who deserves such a privilege! [*Laughs*]

BOWIE: The sub-headline there! [*Laughs*]

McQUEEN: Oh my God no, 'cause I'm an atheist and an anti-royalist, so why would I put anyone on a pedestal?

BOWIE: Well, it does draw one's attention back to your clothes, and what you do is actually more important than anything else.

McQUEEN: Well, I think it would limit your lifestyle somewhat if you said your music is just for that person down the road.

BOWIE: You just sort of hope there's someone out there that might like what you do.

McQUEEN: And there's always someone, I mean the world is such a big place.

BOWIE: Yeah. Prodigy or Oasis?

McQUEEN: Prodigy. I think they're brilliant.

BOWIE: Well, you haven't answered this one. I have to drag you out on this one. Armani or Versace? [*Laughs*]

McQUEEN: Marks and Spencer. I'm sorry. I don't see the relevance of the two of them put together. Actually, they should have amalgamated and sort of formed one company out of both. If you can imagine the rhinestones on one of them deconstructed suits . . .

BOWIE: What do you eat?

McQUEEN: What do I eat?

BOWIE: Yeah.

McQUEEN: Well, I've just had a guinea fowl today . . . it was quite an occasion to come here . . . It's such a lovely place and I love to come here. Bryan Ferry comes here a lot. It's an amazing place and it was built in the Arts and Crafts Movement by Isabella's husband's grandfather. It's on a hill in Gloucestershire and it overlooks Wales and everything. And my bedroom is decorated with Burne-Jones's *Primavera* tapestry—I always come here to get away.

BOWIE: So this is your sanctuary is it?

McQUEEN: Yes, it is. Very much so.

BOWIE: Did you ever have an affair with anyone famous?

McQUEEN: Not famous, but from a very rich family. Very rich Parisian family.

BOWIE: Did you find it an easy relationship, or was it filled with conflicts?

McQUEEN: No, it . . . he was the most wonderful person I have ever met and I was completely honest with him. Never hushed my background or where I came from, and this was when I was only nineteen or twenty, I went out with him and I said to him whatever we do, we do it Dutch and he didn't understand what I said. He thought it was a form of sexual technique! Going Dutch!! [*Laughs*] I said it means paying for each of us separately. He thought that was great, but he gave the best blow job ever! [*Laughter*]

BOWIE: How royal! Was it old money or was it industrial wealth?

McQUEEN: Longtime industrial aristocratic wealth.

BOWIE: Do you go abroad very much? I mean just for yourself, not for work?

McQUEEN: No, not really.

BOWIE: So you really are happy in your homegrown environment?

McQUEEN: I like London, but I love Scotland! I'd never been to Aberdeen before and I went to see Murray's friends in Aberdeen for the first time and it was unreal because I stepped off the plane and I just felt like I belonged there. It's very rare that I do that because I have been to most places in the world, like most capital cities in Japan and America, and you feel very hostile when you step off the plane in these places. I stepped off the plane in Aberdeen and I felt like I've lived there all my life. And it's a really weird sensation. I like more of the Highlands. My family originated from Skye.

BOWIE: Are you a good friend, a stand-up guy, or a flake?

McQUEEN: I'm afraid I have very few friends and I think that all of the friends I have I can depend on and they can depend on me. I don't have hangers-on, and I'm very aggressive to people that if I read through 'em in a second, they've usually found the wrong person to deal with. So if you have got me as a friend, you've got me for life. And I'd do anything for them, but I don't really have associates that use me or abuse me, unless I ask them to! [*Laughs*]

BOWIE: Are you excited about taking over at Givenchy?

McQUEEN: I am and I'm not. To me, I'm sort of saving a sinking ship and not because of John Galliano, but because of the house. It doesn't really seem to know where it's going at the moment and, at the end of the day, they've got to depend on great clothes, not the great name.

BOWIE: Have you already formulated a kind of direction you want to take them?

McQUEEN: Yeah, I have.

BOWIE: Is it exciting?

McQUEEN: Yeah it is, because the philosophy is mainly based on someone I really respected in fashion. There's a certain way fashion should go for a house of that stature, not McQueen bumsters, I'm afraid.

BOWIE: My last question. Will you have time to be making my clothes for next year's tour? [*Laughs*]

McQUEEN: Yeah, I will. We should get together. I mean, I want to see you this time. [*Laughs*]

BOWIE: We could put this on the record right now . . . are you going to make it over here for the VH-1 Fashion Awards? I can't remember.

McQUEEN: When is it?

BOWIE: October 24th or something . . .

McQUEEN: My fashion show is on the 22nd.

BOWIE: So you're probably not going to make it. 'Cause you know I am wearing the Union jacket on that. Because millions of people deserve to see it.

McQUEEN: You've got to say, "This is by McQueen!" [*Laughs*]

BOWIE: Gail will be wearing all her clobber as well.

McQUEEN: Oh, she's fab!

BOWIE: Oh, she wears it so well.

McQUEEN: I'd love to do your tour clothes for you again.

BOWIE: Oh, well that's great. I can't wait to be properly fitted up this time!

McQUEEN: Yeah, definitely. But I've got to see you. I don't want wrist measurements over the phone, 'cause I'm sure you lie about your waist measurements as well! [*Laughs*]

BOWIE: No, not at all . . .

McQUEEN: 'Cause you know some people lie about their length! [*Laughs*]

BOWIE: I just said I'd never lie about the inside leg measurement.

McQUEEN: What side do you dress David, left or right? [*Laughs*]

BOWIE: Both!

McQUEEN: Yeah, right.

BOWIE: No. Yes. Well, maybe.

BUST'S INTERVIEW WITH DAVID BOWIE

INTERVIEW BY IMAN
BUST MAGAZINE
FALL 2000

David Bowie is a prince among men, a man whose myriad talents and enduring beauty make you wonder if he really did fall to Earth from some other, more highly evolved planet. So when we discovered that his wife, Iman, was a fan of BUST magazine (she has a very flattering link from her I-IMAN cosmetics website), we were all over her like brown on rice, begging her to allow us access to her husband for our Men We Love issue. The ethereal Iman then did the unthinkable— she granted our wish. There was only one catch; she wanted to interview David herself. And she wanted us to write the questions.

So, write we did. Iman then handpicked which of our questions she would ask her hubby, and delivered a completely transcribed interview to our email box by the next week. The results are what you see here. Although the couple seem to have rejected most of our questions (including, "What exactly did you mean by 'Suffragette City'?"), their willingness to take even a few moments out of their glamorous lives on behalf of BUST left us feeling like we'd been graced by royalty. Really.

•   •   •

BUST: What does the word *feminism* mean to you?

BOWIE: Not too much anymore, I'm afraid. I've always had immense problems with "movements" or indeed, anything that can be put in quotes. Whatever the current manifesto, the personal definition is always subjective, which is, at the core, the greater reality. In general, I suppose, I find it intensely offensive to see women treated as chattel or appendages. I cannot think of a situation where a woman could not do an equal if not better job than a man. Possibly, a situation requiring only brute strength may be the exception, but here again, a woman would be smart enough to organize the right person for the job. In that singular case, probably a man.

BUST: Do you consider yourself a feminist?

BOWIE: No. I'm stubbornly a nothing-ist. *ists* and *isms* irk me. It's a British trait, I fear. We have a traditionally ambivalent outlook on social movements of any kind. But as with all ambivalence it has produced a kind of schizoid overview. A generous acceptance of eccentricity and, at times, an overbearing need to not stand out as being different. A complete understanding of the individual to command his or her own freedom yet a crushing failure to produce a jolly good revolution, even with Tom Paine at the helm.

BUST: In "When You're a Boy" you sang about the glory of being young and male. Do you think there is a similar glory to being young and female?

BOWIE: The glory in that song was ironic. I do not feel that there is anything remotely glorious about being either male or female. I was merely playing on the idea of the colonization of a gender.

BUST: Is it better to be one or the other?

BOWIE: That is, in my opinion, an absurd question.

BUST: What do you think about machismo?

BOWIE: If you mean Sly Stallone, not very much. Thoroughly silly. If Trevor Howard, then most agreeable.

BUST: Do you consider yourself macho in any way?

BOWIE: I could survive in a jungle and I have to shave once a day. Will that do? I think to consider oneself macho is already a signal that one isn't too sure of oneself.

BUST: Do you have any close male friends?

BOWIE: Not too many close friends, really. About half a dozen that I would think of as close in the accepted sense, i.e., Would I reach out to them in a time of real crisis? Would they reach out to me? The males among that group all go back to my teenage years. Very longstanding friendships. I believe

I am a friendly and fairly outgoing person, but I am slow to make close friendships, male or female.

BUST: Why do men shy away from being glamorous?

BOWIE: I have no time for glamour. It seems a ridiculous thing to strive for. I couldn't care less. A clean pair of shoes should serve quite well enough.

BUST: What didn't you like about Iman at first, that you've grown to love?

BOWIE: The fact that one in four telephone conversations was conducted in Somali, Arabic, or Italian. I found it frustrating that I had no idea what she was talking to her friends and family about. Being British, I expect everyone to converse in English. It was something of a rude awakening. Now I enjoy trying to figure out the odd word and I make up my own imagined subject matter.

BUST: Of you and Iman, who's the better cook?

BOWIE: Well, I burn water. Iman is a superb cook. Our son and daughter both cook very well. I am stricken with shame that I never bothered to learn. Oh, I could boil an egg. And make radioactive coffee.

BUST: What do you think makes relationships between men and women work?

BOWIE: Complete and absolute generosity with the duvet. The realization that the differences between you will be the key to love, as they will become more apparent as the relationship grows. These are the things to be treasured above all else. The similarities will take care of themselves.

AS THE ARTIST SAID TO THE ROCK STAR . . .

CONVERSATION WITH TRACEY EMIN
THE GUARDIAN
JULY 18, 2001

When David Bowie decided to set up a virtual gallery for art students, he began an email discussion with Tracey Emin about art, drugs, and fame. This is an edited transcript of their correspondence.

BOWIE: I am a brand-new art student from Surrey. I would like to break into the art world. Could you give me some tips please?

EMIN: You're not a brand-new art student from Surrey, you're David Bowie! But if you were, I would say get a good part-time job. If you can't afford a studio, always carry a camera and a notebook. If your brain feels a bit dead, enroll in a part-time course—maybe philosophy, a language, or art history—but whatever you do don't think the world owes you a living.

BOWIE: What are you wearing right now? (And don't lie, because I can see you.)

EMIN: I'm wearing an Adidas zip-up tracksuit top from 1996, a pair of Helmut Lang jeans that are two sizes too big for me, a pair of smashed-up old loafers, a black nylon slip from M&S, expensive underwear from Agent Provocateur, a pair of blue Calvin Klein sunglasses, a clear plastic Swatch watch, a fair bit of gold jewelry, and no makeup. Today is a working day.

BOWIE: Does your work point to a "truth"?

EMIN: With my work I'm always credited with the truth, but of course everything I do is edited, considered, and its final production very much calculated. But that doesn't make me fake.

BOWIE: Does it matter if you lie? As you say, your work is often edited and manipulated to produce a certain perspective. If all our truths are based on a series of spiraling misrepresentations, are we then left with searching for some mysterious logos of our own devising? A kind of "gut feeling" for truth? Aren't we just creating truth as a survival tactic?

EMIN: "Surely god will look the other way today"—ring any bells? Yes, it's true most of us use truth when it suits us. I know when I've fucked up, I know when I've hurt people, I know when I've behaved outrageously. A lot of my life has been fucked up but even an idiot can see it's getting better and better. The strange thing is that all the major mistakes that I've made in my life have been decisions fueled by alcohol, mainly vast amounts of whisky. I haven't drunk spirits since September 1999.

BOWIE: Do you think more about the history of art now that you're a household name than when you were just a Margate name?

EMIN: I've never been really good on the history of art and I've never really studied it. I didn't go to the Tate gallery until I was twenty-two—I didn't even know where it was—but I got into Egon Schiele when I was fourteen because your LP cover for *Lodger* was inspired by Schiele. From then on I took an interest in German expressionism. But I don't think anyone is going to be a successful artist by parodying something that has gone before.

BOWIE: I would have to disagree with you. I think so much well-known work over the last ten years or so has been a re-statement of earlier stuff. Everyone from Nauman and Beuys to Koons and Richter has been raided and pillaged. On the shoulders of giants, etc. Although what's been just as fascinating is the reluctance of many observers to credit the original pieces where it might have been appropriate or illuminating.

EMIN: I once quoted to you the line from *The Man Who Fell to Earth* where you say to your driver, "Slow down, Arthur." At the time you said you had no memory of this line; you were on uppers, downers, a concoction of drugs just to keep you going. Do you think being "out of it" adds to the creative process, or is this a myth? I mean, Van Gogh and absinthe, Victorian writers and opium, rock stars and cocaine.

BOWIE: Mmm . . . having experienced drugs, the work is

never the same again. *Station to Station* was a drug album. *Low* and *"Heroes"* were not. *Never Let Me Down* was. It's all contradictory.

EMIN: Mr. Newton, the character you played in *The Man Who Fell to Earth*, was obsessed with channel hopping, invention, and mass-media communication. Don't you see eerie similarities between Mr. Newton and you now?

BOWIE: It was Nic Roeg's intention to show that Newton's only means of collecting and sifting data was channel hopping. This, to me, intimates that he had at least some interest in what was going on around him. At that point I'm not sure that I had quite the same passion for "reality" as he. My preferred viewing was the "snow" on the spare channel. My "truth" was somewhere between extraterrestrial magi and a few good grams.

EMIN: You've been involved with projects on the Net right from the beginning. Is this due to your superstar status? I'm sure it's difficult for David Bowie to pop down to the shops and buy a newspaper, so is the Net a good way of keeping in touch with life on an everyday level?

BOWIE: "Difficult to pop down the shops?" Blimey, Trace! It's delightful and yet a bit worrying that you are as much a victim of the Tabloid Nation as anyone else. I must really scrutinize your work a little more thoroughly. After all the front pages and column inches that you have engendered, is it really a problem for you to pop down the shops? For me, living in downtown

New York and without the all-pervading British press on twenty-four-hour call, it's a nonexistent problem. "Popping out" is carried out several times a day hereabouts, though of course I do find it expedient to have a train of Lincoln town cars following me at a crawl in case I get a sore ankle.

EMIN: Are you being serious? That's what my New York gallerist said when I asked if David Bowie was famous in New York. I'm glad things are cool for you in New York because when I was in Dublin with you and Iman queuing for the Book of Kells, people were almost fainting on the spot. You once said the best way to travel in London is on public transport: all you have to do is wear a hat and read a Greek newspaper. So what disguise are you wearing today, David? Don't lie, because I can see you.

BOWIE: I'm wearing my heart on my sleeve.

EMIN: Did you always want fame? Is it something you'd wish on your children?

BOWIE: I certainly fancied my own spoonful of it when I was young. I was more than downcast to find that fame brought nothing more than good seats in a restaurant. There is nothing there to covet. The nature of fame seems to have shifted recently. I understand that it doesn't even get you a Madonna ticket these days. So I won't be recommending it to my offspring. Having influence is more rewarding for feeding ego. Satisfaction and excitement with one's work is the biggest buzz, though.

EMIN: Your daughter is almost a year old now. Being a new father at your age, how do you think this is going to affect your "golden years"?

BOWIE: She's already affected them. The added dimension to life, of course, is inescapable. Thinking for and on Alex's behalf. Trying to second-guess how she will develop. Continually looking for ways that I can help her. All that.

EMIN: Throughout my life your music has had a big influence on me. I remember at the age of fourteen vomiting at the end of "Rock 'n' Roll Suicide" after drinking a bottle of sherry, and in later years sailing down the Nile listening to *Young Americans* on a Walkman full blast.

BOWIE: I also remember vomiting at the end of "Rock 'n' Roll Suicide." I remember vomiting at the end of quite a few songs.

EMIN: I've always considered you an artist, not a musician. Why is it so important for you to carry on making visual works?

BOWIE: I usually make work for a specified space. I want something to go in such and such an area of this or that room. A gallery only needs ten pieces—six paintings and four sculptures, say. I make work to fill a gap. That could also be metaphysical. It's a kind of interior decoration. I don't know if that's art. I'm not driven.

EMIN: Now that you are using your website, Bowieart.com, to promote young artists, does it worry you that your name is an instant endorsement for these people? Are you sure that they believe in what they are doing and are not relying too much upon your faith?

BOWIE: Well, you know the Goldsmiths artists, for instance, who are now represented on our site. Do you think they believe in what they do? How much is merely self-advertisement, how much is heartfelt? I would imagine a little of both. Most of the work itself is good. As for my participation and endorsement, I am very proud of the fact that our site gives new artists a showcase and a way to sell their work without their having to pay any commissions. I find also that endorsement is a huge part of creating the artist these days, don't you think? Whether it's patronage or newspaper coverage, it pretty much amounts to who can shout loudest.

THE LAST
INTERVIEW

BBC *EXTRAS*
SEPTEMBER 2006

To promote his appearance on the BBC sitcom Extras, *starring Ricky Gervais, Bowie did an interview that was interspliced with brief snippets from the show of him playing himself on the show, writing a song about the Gervais character with the rest of the cast watching . . .*

BOWIE: What made me want to do a British sitcom? Well, as you probably know, my background's in serious acting, before I started doing the writing-singing thing. And so something like doing *Extras* is a piece of cake for me, really. And it was fun working with Rick, showing him pointers, maybe new ways of approaching comedy that he hadn't really thought about before, I think.

[*Cut away to* Extras *scene*]

[*Bowie at the piano singing*] *He's so depressed at being hated, Fatty takes his own life . . .* Fatty? Fatso?

GERVAIS: Fatty?

ASHLEY JENSEN: Fatso, I like Fatso.

BOWIE: Yeah, let's go with Fatso.

INTERVIEW

BOWIE: When we came up with the idea of doing a song, he said he would do the lyrics with Stephen [Merchant], and I said that would be great, I'd love that to happen, and I'd do the melody, but then I'd give him some jokes for future episodes of *Extras*.

So, I gave him a couple of my better things. There's, there's one [*laughs*] that I think he's doing in the Sir Ian McKellen show, it's, um—"Yeah? You and whose army?" [*Laughs*] Which you know is like, that's an example of the kind of thing that I've got, and there were a couple more— uh, "If you keep looking like that your face will stay like it!" [*Laughs*] That's really quite a zinger, isn't it?

And those kind of things, so you know, I've been writing jokes for him and he assures me they'll be in the future episodes, so it's been very fulfilling, this whole experience.

[Extras *scene*]

[*Bowie singing at the piano, surrounded by the cast and crew of* Extras]

He's banal, and facile,
He's a fat waste of space
See his pug-nose face
Pug, pug
Pug, pug (again!)
See his pug nose face, yeeaaah
Pug pug
Pug pug . . .

[*Fade out*]

DAVID BOWIE was born David Jones in the working-class London neighborhood of Brixton on January 8, 1947. His mother was a waitress, and his father worked at a children's charity. As a boy, he played ukulele and bass in skiffle bands with friends before taking up the saxophone at the inspiration of his half-brother, the jazz musician Terry Burns. In the early 1960s, he switched to guitar and formed a series of rock bands, including the Konrads and the King Bees. But he didn't achieve fame, or even much success, until he became a solo artist and the title track from his second album, "Space Oddity," became a hit in 1969. By that time he'd changed his name to Bowie to avoid confusion with the popular lead singer of the Monkees, Davey Jones. Bowie would go on to become a founder of the "glam rock" school of music, posing as the character Ziggy Stardust, but he would abandon that eventually for a continuing series of dramatic explorations of other styles of music and theatricality over the ensuing decades. Bowie also had a notable career as an actor, starring in such films as *The Man Who Fell to Earth*, and the Broadway play *The Elephant Man*. He kept making records throughout, culminating in *Black Star*, his twenty-seventh album, released on his sixty-ninth birthday, and two days before his death on January 10, 2016.

DENNIS JOHNSON is the publisher of Melville House.

CLIFF MICHELMORE, CBE, was an English broadcast journalist, producer, and talk show host best known for the BBC television program *Tonight*, which he hosted from 1957 to 1965. He died in 2016.

PATRICK SALVO was a rock journalist for several major music publications, including *Rolling Stone* and *Melody Maker*, in addition to *Interview*. He was the coauthor of *The Authorized 1972 Rolling Stones Tour Book*, and head writer for the television show about the seminal sixties radio DJ The Real Don Steele. He died in 2005.

CRAIG COPETAS has been a reporter or editor for numerous notable publications, including *Rolling Stone, Esquire, The Wall Street Journal, Bloomberg News*, and others, covering everything from rock and roll to the 2003 invasion of Iraq, when he was in the first wave of embedded reporters. He's also the author of several books, including *Mona Lisa's Pajamas: Diverting Dispatches from a Roving Reporter*.

KURT LODER was a longtime reporter for *Rolling Stone* before becoming news director at MTV, with which he remains affiliated. He's also the author of several books, including collections of his film reviews and stories from *Rolling Stone*. He also coauthored Tina Turner's autobiography *I, Tina*, then later contributed to the screenplay for the movie based on the book, *What's Love Got to Do with It?*

VIRGINIA CAMPBELL was editor in chief of *Movieline*.

ALEXANDER MCQUEEN was a British fashion designer and couturier best known for being chief designer at Givenchy before founding his own successful label. He won the British Fashion Designer of the Year Award four times (1996, 1997, 2001, and 2003). He also designed the wardrobe for David Bowie's tours in the late 1990s. McQueen committed suicide in 2010 at age forty.

IMAN was born Zara Mohamed Abdulmajid in Mogadishu, Somalia. She was discovered by fashion photographer Peter Beard while still a college student, and had a long career as a top international model before launching her own cosmetics line and turning to philanthropic endeavors. She has acted in numerous films, including the Oscar-winning *Out of Africa*, as well as *Star Trek VI*. She married David Bowie in 1992.

TRACEY EMIN, CBE, is a contemporary British artist known for her confrontational and confessional style across several mediums, including painting, sculpture, photography, and installation art. She first came to fame as one of the Young British Artists group—or Britart—of the 1980s. She is one of only two women to have ever been appointed a professor at the Royal Academy of Arts since its founding in 1768.

RICKY GERVAIS began his career as a singer in the 1980s New Wave band Seona Dancing, and as manager of the band Suede, before turning to stand-up comedy. In 2001, he created, cowrote, codirected, and starred in the TV show *The Office*, which was his breakout show in both the United States and the UK. In addition to acting in numerous movies, he has had several hit television shows since then, including *Extras*, *An Idiot Abroad*, and *Derek*.

THE LAST INTERVIEW SERIES

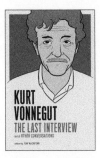

KURT VONNEGUT: THE LAST INTERVIEW

"I think it can be tremendously refreshing if a creator of literature has something on his mind other than the history of literature so far. Literature should not disappear up its own asshole, so to speak."

$15.95 / $17.95 CAN
978-1-61219-090-7
ebook: 978-1-61219-091-4

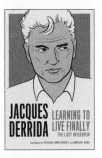

LEARNING TO LIVE FINALLY: THE LAST INTERVIEW
JACQUES DERRIDA

"I am at war with myself, it's true, you couldn't possibly know to what extent . . . I say contradictory things that are, we might say, in real tension; they are what construct me, make me live, and will make me die."

translated by PASCAL-ANNE BRAULT and MICHAEL NAAS

$15.95 / $17.95 CAN
978-1-61219-094-5
ebook: 978-1-61219-032-7

ROBERTO BOLAÑO: THE LAST INTERVIEW

"Posthumous: It sounds like the name of a Roman gladiator, an unconquered gladiator. At least that's what poor Posthumous would like to believe. It gives him courage."

translated by SYBIL PEREZ and others

$15.95 / $17.95 CAN
978-1-61219-095-2
ebook: 978-1-61219-033-4

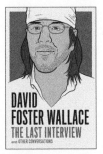

DAVID FOSTER WALLACE: THE LAST INTERVIEW

"I don't know what you're thinking or what it's like inside you and you don't know what it's like inside me. In fiction . . . we can leap over that wall itself in a certain way."

$15.95 / $15.95 CAN
978-1-61219-206-2
ebook: 978-1-61219-207-9

THE LAST INTERVIEW SERIES

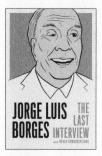

JORGE LUIS BORGES: THE LAST INTERVIEW

"Believe me: the benefits of blindness have been greatly exaggerated. If I could see, I would never leave the house, I'd stay indoors reading the many books that surround me."

translated by KIT MAUDE

$15.95 / $15.95 CAN
978-1-61219-204-8
ebook: 978-1-61219-205-5

HANNAH ARENDT: THE LAST INTERVIEW

"There are no dangerous thoughts for the simple reason that thinking itself is such a dangerous enterprise."

$15.95 / $15.95 CAN
978-1-61219-311-3
ebook: 978-1-61219-312-0

RAY BRADBURY: THE LAST INTERVIEW

"You don't have to destroy books to destroy a culture. Just get people to stop reading them."

$15.95 / $15.95 CAN
978-1-61219-421-9
ebook: 978-1-61219-422-6

JAMES BALDWIN: THE LAST INTERVIEW

"You don't realize that you're intelligent until it gets you into trouble."

$15.95 / $15.95 CAN
978-1-61219-400-4
ebook: 978-1-61219-401-1

THE LAST INTERVIEW SERIES

GABRIEL GÁRCIA MÁRQUEZ: THE LAST INTERVIEW

"The only thing the Nobel Prize is good for is not having to wait in line."

$15.95 / $15.95 CAN
978-1-61219-480-6
ebook: 978-1-61219-481-3

LOU REED: THE LAST INTERVIEW

"Hubert Selby. William Burroughs. Allen Ginsberg. Delmore Schwartz . . . I thought if you could do what those writers did and put it to drums and guitar, you'd have the greatest thing on earth."

$15.95 / $15.95 CAN
978-1-61219-478-3
ebook: 978-1-61219-479-0

ERNEST HEMINGWAY: THE LAST INTERVIEW

"The most essential gift for a good writer is a built-in, shockproof, shit detector."

$15.95 / $20.95 CAN
978-1-61219-522-3
ebook: 978-1-61219-523-0

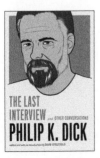

PHILIP K. DICK: THE LAST INTERVIEW

"The basic thing is, how frightened are you of chaos? And how happy are you with order?"

$15.95 / $20.95 CAN
978-1-61219-526-1
ebook: 978-1-61219-527-8

THE LAST INTERVIEW SERIES

NORA EPHRON: THE LAST INTERVIEW

"You better *make* them care about what you think.
It had better be quirky or perverse or thoughtful
enough so that you hit some chord in them. Otherwise,
it doesn't work."

$15.95 / $20.95 CAN
978-1-61219-524-7
ebook: 978-1-61219-525-4

JANE JACOBS: THE LAST INTERVIEW

"I would like it to be understood that all our human
economic achievements have been done by ordinary
people, not by exceptionally educated people, or by
elites, or by supernatural forces."

$15.95 / $20.95 CAN
978-1-61219-534-6
ebook: 978-1-61219-535-3